I dedicate this book to the fallen men of the North Staffordshire Regiment who fell during the Great War.

ACKNOWLEDGMENTS

Many people have contributed in the process of producing this study of the North Staffordshire Regiment. Writing this book would have been so difficult without the kindness and generosity of those who have helped to piece together this book.

A big thank you is owed to Andrew Thornton BA Hons History and war studies. Andrew has shared a wealth of Information on the attack on the Hohenzollern Redoubt in which his own Great Grandfather Took part. Andrew has devoted much of his working life to the study of the North Staffordshire Regiment. Andrew also has an MPhil in Modern History but this is based entirely on his own thesis on the Staffordshire Territorials. Andrew is also an Honorary Research Fellow of the centre for First World War Studies at the University of Birmingham.

Thank you to Jonathan Honeysett MBE, who has supported me and provided me with information from his own work, in Reference to the German Artillery used during the Great War and for sharing his father's experiences with me.

I would also like to thank the Sentinel, especially Colette Warbrook, who published my first letter to the Sentinel asking for help from any local descendants of the Fallen. Without Colette's help this book would not be what it is today.

Gillian and Alan Talbot, Old Kit Bag LLP who supplied the information on the Uttoxeter men

The following people helped me with my book by replying to my Sentinel advertisement.

Elaine Clayton

Trixie Bennett

Trevor Davenhill

Paul Dyer

Sue Giles

Susan Lawton

David Malkin

Lynn Ormston

Phil Rowley

David Smith

Simon Wakeling

Mark Watson

And of course the 95 year old lady who emailed me information on her relative George Coomer, who wishes to remain anonymous.

Thank you to the research team at the Staffordshire Regiment museum, for sending me information on the various campaigns the Staffords took part in during the Great War.

Also many thanks to my Parents John Chevin and Tracey Hughes who have supported me with my project, and last but by no means least my friends who have supported me and followed my progress on social media sites such as Facebook.

Foreword.

As this is my first book I have written I think it is only right I introduce myself to you, the reader. My name is Callan Chevin. I was born on February 24th 1992 and spent my childhood in Longton. Admittedly I loved going to school, and from an early age it was clear I enjoyed learning. My life has been far from easy, from birth I had complications. I underwent heart surgery in 1992 and spent 9 months in intensive care. The local paper The Sentinel, which will frequently appear in this book dubbed me the baby with 9 lives. All seemed well until I reached high school and I started to grow. I kept developing lung infections it was making me bad and felt unable to interact with fellow class mates. Anyhow in 2011 the source of the problem was found and when I was 19 I had to have yet more surgery. It went terribly wrong and again I found myself in intensive care yet again. I spent 6 weeks in Birmingham hospital. After my recovery I returned back to Staffordshire University and graduated in 2013 with a 2:2 in BA Hons Modern History.

That's my medical over and done with, now let's get into the education. I must firstly say my passion for the Great War has been a gradual development but one that never ceases to amaze, shock and at times upset me. From an early age I have loved to learn about the past. Admittedly my interests have changed over time. In school I loved the Ancient Romans. This developed into an interest in Tudor life, especially in our capital, London. In 2012, my interests changed to that of the Regency period, I seemed to love the pomp and vanity of the Georgian monarchs, such as that of King George IV. However throughout my life Military History has been a main focal point. The Second World War, the politics, the horror of the Third Reich and above all the Holocaust grabbed my attention. My passion for the Great War came by chance when I enquired to a Facebook history page about a medal I inherited. The medal is a Victory Medal and was my Great Great Grandfathers, Alfred Sanders. To my astonishment I was told he served at Gallipoli, the Somme and further research showed me he had a cousin, also called Alfred Sanders who was taken prisoner in 1917. The fact they served in the North and South Staffordshire Regiments woke up a sense of local pride inside me, and I decided to look up more. Studying my past further I found three more Great War relatives, one of which was a private John Chevin, my Great Grandfather who served in the 5th Battalion of the North Staffordshire Regiment. It was here in around 2013 I encountered the attack on the Hohenzollern redoubt on October 13th 1915. This event has remained strongly in my mind ever since. Looking at books regarding the Battle of Loos I felt disappointed how little was mentioned about the North

Stafford's, in most books they are collectively included with the 46th midland division. This is correct however I felt something had to be done to study the fallen men of Staffordshire as individuals. It was then I decided to study this particular day, Wednesday October 13th 1915, Staffordshire's blackest day.

Callan Chevin.

Contents:

Introduction: 1 - 28

Chapter one: The Battle of   Loos. 32 - 66

Chapter two: Potters forever! Accounts of the slaughter. 67 - 207

Chapter three: The fallen men of North Staffordshirand help From present day potters. 208 – 340

Chapter four: The short life of Ernest Godfrey Thomas. 341 – 385

Chapter 5 Remembrance in the Staffordshire area 386 - 424

Roll of honour 426 - 496

Introduction

Whilst at work one day at the local hospital a young patient expressed his interest too me in history. He told me of his interest in the Tudors and all the gruesome things such as executions, and the Plague. My self being somewhat older than this young man thought I would share my interests with him. I told him one day I would like to write a book, about an event that affected the people of Staffordshire nearly one hundred years ago. He seemed relatively interested for a boy of his age but the nurse caring for him asked me more, so I explained. She couldn't believe the fact over 500 men from Staffordshire were killed or wounded in just one hour. Her exact words were I feel rather disgusted I never knew that.

The fact is that she wasn't the only person who didn't know about Staffordshire's blackest day, it seemed hardly anyone did. It had seemed that history had forgotten this day and it had been over taken by the massive offensives that took place in 1916 and 1917, them being the Somme and the Third Ypres, more commonly known as Passchendaele. The North Staffordshire Regiment had seen action in the majority of the campaigns of the Great War. An approximate total of 13,000 men were either killed or wounded during the Great War from Staffordshire or who had links to Stoke on Trent according to the Commonwealth War Graves Commission. It would have been impossible for anyone in Staffordshire and Stoke on Trent not to have known anyone who was killed or wounded a century ago. This certainly echoes today and many more people have taken an interest in looking into their family history.

The Battle of Loos, pronounced Los that was fought from September 25th 1915 to October 13th 1915 is a rather unstudied area of the Great War. The area known as the Western Front is a pilgrimage for thousands of people, who every year go to remember and pay their respects to their fallen ancestors. The two main areas visited are the Ypres salient and of course the battlefields surrounding the river Somme. The locals readily welcome them, both to educate but also to make money, by enticing them in to their hotels and cafes. There is an area of land between Ypres and the Somme that gets much less attention from tourists. The two areas mentioned were of course once places of terrible destruction and a never ending source of death and misery for our long gone British heroes. The area of Loos now looks like any part of the Western Front, farm land, however is noticeably flatter than the rest of the Front. The men who fell at Loos have far from been forgotten, there are memorials in the area, but tourists are hurried through this flat landscape to see the main "attraction" to the south, the Somme and the Theipval.

Before we move on to the main topic of this book I think it is important to acknowledge a few of the other conflicts in which the North Staffordshire Regiment took part in during the Great War. The Battle of Gallipoli, Neuve Chapelle, The Somme, Lens and St Quentin.

On April 25th 1915 the Gallipoli campaign began. Although it is remembered every year in Australia and New Zealand as ANZAC day, the British contribution is sometimes over looked. The British were there from the beginning alongside our colonial brethren's and many others drafted in to help the ANZAC's in July 1915. In terms of local

Staffordshire men, it was the 7th Battalion of the North Staffordshire Regiment who served here.

In my search for my own family History the Research team at the Staffordshire Regiment museum kindly sent me some information on the Gallipoli Campaign which will hopefully give a better insight into this disastrous campaign.

The Dardanelles was to be the scene of the 7th Battalion's debut in the front line. Final leave having been granted, the Battalion re-assembled and moved to Avonmouth where it embarked on transports on June 20th 1915 and sailed 1100 strong with 28 officers. After a smooth passage across the seas, Gibraltar was passed on the 25th and a halt was made at Malta for a day on the 27th. Finally the Battalion arrived in Alexandria where all units disembarked and made a route march through the town. Orders were received for all the Regimental transport to be left there as it could not be landed on the peninsula. After leaving Alexandria the convoy touch at Mudros, the advanced base of the Mediterranean Expeditionary Force and then sailed direct to cape Helles.

The Battalion received its baptism by fire immediately after landing at cape Helles on July 11th 1915. The sea ran red with blood. At the time there was no place on the Gallipoli peninsula where the British were not under artillery fire. So the units of brigades had to provide themselves with cover by means of digging entrenchments as quickly as possible, in the many nullahs and gullies running down the beach and to wait until orders for further movement should arrive.

The situation on the peninsula was one of standstill. The French were on the right, just in advance of a stream called the Kereves Dere while the British on the left had captured the Gully Ravine. All efforts to move forward by capturing the heights of Achi Baba and the village of Krithia had proved abortive, and those in command were beginning to realise that task set before them one which would tax very highly far more troops than they then had available. All units were being used to their uttermost strength.

There was to be no tour of the trenches for the Brigade on the 13th of July it was moved to support the Lowland division, which was attacking Achi Baba. The attack was partially successful, but the 39th Brigade did not move up to the front line and on the 15th they were withdrawn and sent to take over a part of the line from the 28th Division. The North Staffords remained in the line for a fortnight during which the Turks were very active. On the 19th of July they made a desperate attack which was driven off. On July 20th the 28th division took over the line again and the brigade moved down to the beach, embarked on lighters and proceed to Mudros on the 31st for a short rest.

On August 4th orders were issued for the attempt to force a new landing at Suvla bay and the Brigade embarked on the 5th to sail to ANZAC to take part in operations. The Battalions memories of the first day at ANZAC are anything but pleasant. Landing at dawn from lighters they advanced over very open ground under and intense and accurate barrage from the Turkish guns. Orders were given to dig at once, and the Brigade remained there until nightfall. The low-lying country by the sea was completely overlooked by the enemy on the heights of Sari Bair and they were able to inform their front line and their artillery of all movements and dispositions. The ground was devoid of cover and any moment in the open was certain to bring disaster. It was almost impossible to take any ammunition, food or water to the front line and equally impossible to evacuate any wounded. It was marvellous that the British troops were able to hold on as long as they did.

During the last weeks of summer the swarms of flies brought disease, as well as pestering the troops for any moisture from their eyes or from what little food and drink they had. The smell of the latrines became unbearable and so did they dead they were unable to bury. The British were not expecting the harsh Turkish winter where temperatures plunged well below zero, many suffered from frost bite and moral was at an all-time low, and with all of this the fighting still continued into January 1916.

The Gallipoli campaign was a complete disaster, and led to an evacuation of all army personnel in early 1916. This campaign had cost Britain and her empire 250,000 casualties.

A breakdown of cemeteries reveals some of those North Stafford's who fell along the Dardanelles peninsular.

7th field ambulance cemetery. 33 North Stafford's laid to rest.

Green hill cemetery. 5 North Stafford's laid to rest.

Hill 10 cemetery 11 North Stafford's laid to rest

Azmak cemetery. 16 North Stafford's laid to rest.

Redoubt cemetery. 4 North Stafford's laid to rest.

The largest collection of North Stafford's are laid to rest in Helles cemetery, which contains 347 men.

Some of the men of the 7th North Staffordshire Regiment.

[1]

From March 10th-13th 1915 a large battle took place, the battle was situated in and around the town of Neuve Chapelle. The battle saw the losses of 11,000 British men, which included 4,200 Indians fighting for Great Britain. Before the battle the British mounted a huge bombardment. In 35 minutes more shells were dropped on the German lines than the entire number of shells fired during the second Boer war, 1899-1902. An account of this battle exists from a man called Mr Hassell, who survived the battle and who lived in Tunstall in Stoke on Trent.

---

[1] Men of the 7TH Battalion North Staffordshire Regiment, the Staffordshire weekly sentinel Saturday July 17th 1915.

"You will probably heard that my governor was killed in action on the 11th of March. It was great shock. I had only left him about three hours when he fell but I did not hear of his death until 1am. It was a terrible time, Hell in all its hideousness could not be worse. The sights one saw were enough to turn the brain of the strongest. One has heard much of Dante's inferno, but that is a mere detail compared to the four days at Neuve Chappelle. All day long guns were making way for the infantry to get on the move.. Wire entanglements had to be cut, trenches had to be taken during a perfect hurricane of fire both from the enemy's artillery and machine guns. Honestly it is impossible for me to say what really happened. At one hour I saw all my company in high spirits, well and strong, the next, I saw ten percent of them hurled into eternity. As one leaped from one trench to another the cries of the wounded could be heard between the bursts from the guns. For about one and a half miles down the road the shells were continually bursting. I don't think I shall ever forget the sights I saw at the dressing station, or the cries of the wounded. There were English, Indians and Germans on the side of the road."

The article was Published may 1st 1915 In the Sentinel.

The most infamous Battle of the Great War saw the deaths of 227 Staffordshire men who fell on July 1st 1916 was at a northern point of the Battle of the Somme. This area was called Gommecourt. Gommecourt is located about eight miles north of the town called Albert. It was from Albert where the first British troops left the trenches at 07.30 am. As heavy fighting took place around Albert, the troops of the 46th midland division started their offensive. Their aims were to draw some German reserves from the main Somme offensive further south and also to try and eliminate a

German salient here in the lines, which was centred on Gommecourt Wood. The 46th midland was assisted by the 56th division which consisted of men from London. The intention was for troops from the two Divisions to meet and thus 'pinch out' the salient here. The advance of the 56th Division went quite well initially, with the enemy's first two lines taken, but there was more resistance from the third line.

However, the 46th (North Midland) Division did not fare so well. The wire in front of the German trenches had not been cut by the barrage, and although a few men of the 1/6 South Stafford's and 1/6 North Stafford's did get into the enemy's front-line trenches, they and the other attackers here (Battalions of the Sherwood Foresters) had little success and were driven back with significant losses.2

---

[2] http://www.ww1battlefields.co.uk/somme/gommecourt.html

The memorial plaque to the men of the 46th Midland division who fell at Gommecourt.

The research team at the Staffordshire Regiment Museum, kindly sent me some information in the post about the action at Gommecourt, as I was enquiring about my Great Grandfather John Chevin who was in the 1/5th Battalion of the North Staffordshire Regiment and who took part in the action at Gommecourt.

On June 24th the bombardment began, and never ceased, except for half an hour each afternoon, whilst the British aeroplanes went over to take photographs. The Germans did not send many shells back, but carefully registered the communication trenches and cross roads, and put back salvos of heavies into the village. The lot of two companies in reserve in the village was anything but happy. As soon as it was dusk every available man had to turn out to dig assembly trenches and clear the communication trenches. Returning usually wet through at 4 am they were called out again at 9am for various tasks such as pumping water out of the trenches, building dug outs, carrying meals to the front line, with the din of the bombardment always in their ears and shells dropping all around. No wonder they were so tired.

A considerable distance separated the opposing front lines, and it was not until the bombardment had commenced that it was decided to dig to a jumping off trench in front of the British front lines. The 6th North Staffords, who were back at Humbercourt , a mile or two in the rear were detailed to do the digging , while the 5TH North Staffords were to find covering parties.

As mentioned before the preliminary bombardment, which had commenced on June 24th extended all along the British Front as well as the Somme Region. The preparations had not passed unnoticed by the Germans and they were quiet prepared for it. In several trenches they had even hoisted up placards saying "come on we are ready for you"

The bombardment was to continue until the 28th which was the day originally fixed for the opening of the attack. It was the most extensive bombardment up to then and was the fruit of many months of preparation.

The 5th North Staffords waited in the trenches and on June 26th were allowed two days' rest. The great attack had originally been fixed to take place at 7.30 on the morning on June 28th 1916 but on the preceding days the weather had broken and many heavy thunderstorms had filled the trenches with water, and made them almost useless, so it was decided to attack three days later on July 1st.

The aim then of the 46th and 56th divisions, was not so much to take Gommecourt as to prevent its defenders helping in the defence further south.

The article sent to me be the Staffordshire Regiment museum continued with the following. The final artillery preparations began at 6.30 am and was concentrated on the front German trenches. The day dawned hot and cloudless with a thin fog, the result of the damp past week clinging to the hollows. The bombardment lasted until 7.30, when it lifted, and all along the front the British troops went over the top.

Momentarily breaking from the article, it is believed that the troops were ordered to walk over no man's land, this is true but with this description it is easy to see why July 1st 1916 was such a difficult day for the British troops. The average equipment of the soldiers, here and elsewhere consisted of a steel helmet, haversack, water-bottle, rations for two days, two gas helmets, tear goggles, 220 cartridges, two bombs, two sandbag sacks, entrenching tools, and with trenches half full of water, and the ground between a morass of sticky mud some idea can be formed of the strain upon the infantry.

The 5th North Staffords, as soon as the attack commenced were over-whelmed by the German barrage. It especially caught the parties in the communication trenches and as a result they could not advance to help the 6th North Staffords, who were shot down by the machine guns and rifles. A few men and officers reached the German front lines but could do nothing. One man, Lance Corporal R Tivey describes his experience in a letter.

"We went over in broad daylight and in full view of the enemy lines. Attached to my wave would be some 25 men.

We mounted all together keeping extended order line about two yards interval and set off at an easy pace for the next trench. After having proceeded no more than 20 paces, the whole line fell as one man, leaving me running whereupon I was struck for the first time and fell. I did not know what happened really, and surmised the line had been whipped out, since the deliberate rifle fire and maxim fire was concentrated on us. I crawled some yards half left, but my wound was not bad enough to admit returning, so I rose again and ran in quarter circles for the enemy trench. This time shrapnel was bursting and I was the centre of fire. A bullet grazed my thumb and I lost my rifle, another hitting my shrapnel helmet. When within some ten or twenty yards of the enemy wire I was struck again, doubling me up. Close by was a shell hole into which I crawled, the Germans shooting at me when I was down, and hitting the sole of my boot. They turned their Maxim on me and sniped at me if I made a movement. Heavy crumps and mortars were bursting all around. That I did not go mad is more than I can explain away, but I kept remarkably cool. After 12 hours of it I crawled out under the cover of dark and made my way back. This was difficult since my wounds had caught me in the back and stomach and I was bent nearly double"

That is the account of one man but there is one more account that has survived from a man who survived that dreadful day. One man who would prove to be a brilliant source of information on the Battle of Gommecourt was a man called Thomas James Higgins, whose war time diary was published after the Great War. Higgins was not actually called Higgins, in fact his identity is unknown. He was left on the doorstep of a Police Sergeant who lived in Stoke on Trent in 1889, He named him Thomas James Higgins after himself. On the same week 3 babies were found dead in the local canal, it was believed that all these babies were siblings, but it is unknown why this one was kept alive. At the time it was purely believed that because he was a boy he had the best chance of surviving and being taken on by whoever who was left with. The sergeant kept the young boy until he was about 6 but he couldn't afford to keep him as he already had 6 children of his own so put him in a workhouse.

Higgins descriptions of Gommecourt are some of the most vivid battle recollections of the Great War.

July 1st 1916

"In the trench leading to the front line, the sights I saw are impossible to properly describe. The trenches were literally running with blood. The dead and dying lay in heaps at the bottom of the trench. We had to climb over them as we went on"[3]

The next section Higgins describes going over the top.

"FIX BAYONETS! The bullets were whizzing just over the trench and in no man's land the whiz bangs and shells were bursting in hundred's. No one expected to come back again. The officer yelled at the top of his voice, ONE TWO THREE. Over we went with the best of luck. The man next

---

[3] Tommy at Gommecourt. Pp 37

to me named chorlton fell back with a bullet in his head as he was springing over"4

Higgins remembers how lucky he felt to even get over the top of his trench even if too run just a few hundred yards. He recalled that men were falling over like skittles in a game of bowls. Higgins was eventually wounded, at first he thought he broke his back, but it turned out he was rather lucky as he managed to make it back to his trench. His injury was just a scratch compared to the unlucky 20,000 British troops who fell that day. He concluded his coverage of Gommecourt with this diary entry on the evening of July 1st 1916.

"I shall never forget that Saturday, July 1st 1916 if I live to be one hundred. Shells were dropping close to me, chocking me with flumes and dirt. I soon found another danger, Fritz was riddling any poor devil he saw moving with bullets. I moved once and some bullets whizzed past just missing my head! I lay still after that with barbed wire sticking in me, I dare not move. That awful day seemed a life time too me."5

---

[4] Tommy at Gommecourt pp38
[5] Tommy at Gommecourt pp 39

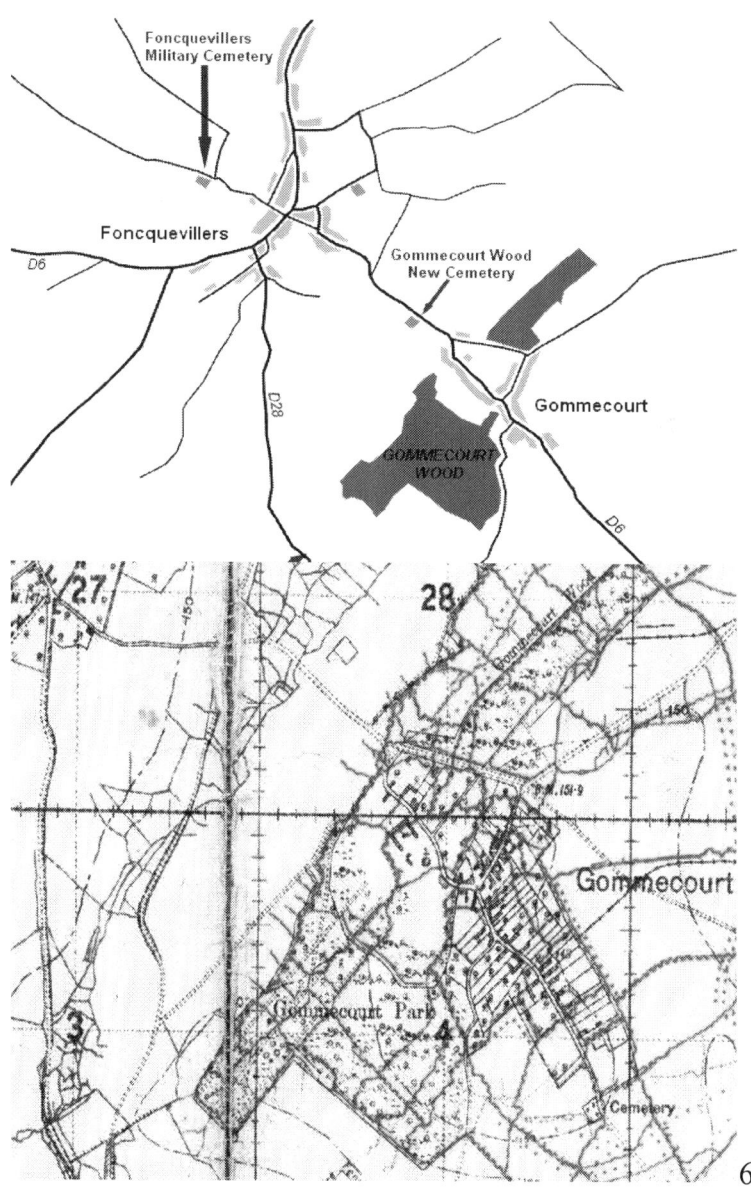

---

[6] http://www.ww1battlefields.co.uk/somme/gommecourt.html both these maps show the modern and the old impression of the site. The

We saw horrendous losses at the Battle of Lens exactly one year after the bloodbath of the Somme on July 1st 1917. The attack was a gamble and completely depended on whether the worn out German division had been replaced or not. The objective was to capture the town of Lens, the first German trench lay inside the town and was heavily wired. This battle as we will later see is rather similar to that of the attack on the Hohenzollern redoubt in terms of the men who took part. The 139th Brigade, the Sherwood's attacked from the left, the 137th brigade in the centre, them being the Stafford's and on the right the 138th Brigade, the Lincolns and Leicester's. This of course made up the 46th Midland Division. It was the 5th Battalion of the North Stafford's who led this charge, followed by the 6th south Stafford's supplying the support. Each man was to carry 150 rounds of ammunition, two days rations and two bombs. Bombers carried eight bombs and rifle grenadiers were equipped with six rifle grenades. The assault commenced at 02.34, a few hours before dawn, trying to use the cover of darkness as protection. At first all seemed to be going well and the first section of barbed wire was breached. To the left the Germans had rushed forward to various machine gun posts. The 5th Stafford's had managed to reach their objective, a trench called Aconite, and their support followed behind clearing the ruined houses of any remaining Germans. The Sherwood's had been unable to reach their objective, thus loosing heavily, the Lincoln's and the Leicester's had been slightly more successful but had not managed to taken the full objective. The main objective, the church had been taken after three attempts. Even though the north Stafford's had managed to capture their objectives, all the officers had been either killed or

---

blue lines on the second image are the British trenches and the red lines are the German Trenches.

wounded. The total losses for the 46th division were 50 officers and 1000 men!

Thomas James Higgins recalls how he realised the date was July 1st, and wondered if this day would be as bad as the year before at Gommecourt. Again he provides a stirring account of the attack on Lens.

"At times like these man is not human. He is changed into a blood thirsty beast. His one desire is to kill. The Germans were mowing down our men by shells and bullets. A man's brains were scattered over the left side of my face and shoulder. I did not notice until the charge was over. Whenever a German came our way he was shot or bayonetted, there was no mercy"[7]

Higgins describes how the dead and dying were lying in heaps all around the town of Lens. Little did he know that this would be his last day of the Great War. Higgins was not killed, but was taken prisoner.

The last slaughter of men from the North Staffordshire Regiment came on March 21st [1918]. After a five hour bombardment near St Quentin. The Germans fired 3.5 million shells ahead of their offensive known as operation Michael. While some preparations were made, the British army was unready for an offensive of the size and scope unleashed by Ludendorff. At 4:35 AM on March 21, German guns opened fire along a 40-mile front.

---

[7] Tommy at Gommecourt pp 78-79

Pummelling the British lines, the barrage caused 7,500 casualties. Advancing, the German assault centred on St. Quentin and the Storm troopers began penetrating the broken British trenches between 6:00 AM and 9:40 AM. Attacking from just north of Arras south to the Oise River, German troops achieved success across the front with the largest advances coming at St. Quentin and in the south. This assault virtually wiped out the 1st Battalion of the North Staffordshire Regiment, and even as it reformed, they lost a further 200 casualties at the Battle of Selle in the last weeks of October 1918.

The reality is that hardly a day passed when a man from Staffordshire didn't die in combat. One of the most useful sources to use when studying the fallen men of Staffordshire is the Sentinel archives. Every week they would issue a copy listing the names and if possible of the photos of the fallen men. Some weeks have more men listed depending on what battle was raging at the time. The casualties would be published the week after the battle took place. One page which is full of photos was published on October 2nd 1915. The battle that began just over a week before was the Battle of Loos on September 25th 1915. In the research these articles would prove to be one of the most useful and reliable sources to hand. The attack on the last day of Loos is not just reflected for one week, not two, not even a month but coverage of the attack on the

Hohenzollern Redoubt continued right into January 1916. At times when compiling the Roll of Honour it seemed rather frustrating that no information of photos could be found, but in many cases the deaths were not confirmed for many months after. One cannot simply imagine the agonizing horror of reading the Evening Sentinel every week and seeing who had fallen over the previous week. In a time where communication was not instant as it is now, the wait to find out whether your son, husband, uncle or any other male relative was alive or dead must have had a gruelling and at times morale deflating effect on the women and children of Staffordshire. Those publications between October 1915 and January 1916 regarding the attack on Hohenzollern must have felt like a never ending nightmare. It is also interesting to note that other than Gallipoli which only has several references, the attack on Hohenzollern also received the most coverage in general. The actual Battle of Loos up until the last day has almost no coverage and is only reflected in the increase of photographs of men who fell during the campaign.

[8] The Staffordshire evening sentinel showing just a few of the fallen potters who fell on September 25th 1915.

---

[8] The Staffordshire evening sentinel, October 2nd 1915.

Song of the Battalion

Hark! Have you heard of the war note, that thrilling trumpet call?

That soundeth out o'er vale and hamlet, o'er hut and lordly hall

Tis mother England calling.

Her sons unto her aid

Then up ye men of Staffordshire, join Blizzards Bold Brigade,

Then up ye men of Staffordshire, join Blizzards Bold Brigade.

There's glory in your banner, there's music in that cheer that rolls along the battle line from the men of Staffordshire.

From Himalaya's summits to Minden's murky plain your colours tell your story, unsmirched by blot or stain.

Then proudly speed the slogan that starts from Trentham hall, and sweeps along the murmuring Trent to distant Caverswall.

Desert be bench and workshop, bereft be wife and maid.

We'll die for dear old England, in Blizzards Bold Brigade.

Chapter One:

The Battle of loos.

"You bloody cowards! Are you leaving me to go alone? Not cowards, sir. Willing enough but they are all f***ing dead!

Lieutenant Robert Graves. Goodbye to all that.

1915 saw the deaths of countless British troops, and it was also one of the worst years of the Great War. Britain failed to complete almost all of her objectives

The biggest offensive of 1915 on the western front was that of Loos. The battle which commenced on September 25th 1915 involved 75,000 men of the British expeditionary force. (BEF) It was the largest single conflict on the western front so far.

There are four main characters involved in this battle. France's General Josef Joffre, Britain's Field marshal John French and Douglas Haig and Germanys General Sixt von Armin,

General Josef Joffre. 12th January 1852 – 3rd January 1931

Joffre was born in 1852 at Rivesaltes in the eastern Pyrenees. He was the son of a cooper and entered the army in 1870 aged eighteen. While still a cadet he showed his leadership potential by taking command of a battery during the Paris Uprising. After this event, he embarked on a number of overseas placements. Joffre served in Indo-China and in North Africa.

While in North Africa, he won distinction in 1894 when, as a lieutenant-colonel, he led a column of men across the North African desert to capture Timbuktu. Between 1904 and 1906, he furthered his career by showing exceptional organisational skills as Director of Engineers. In 1911, he was appointed Chief of the General Staff which meant that he was the senior officer in the French Army when World War One broke out in August 1914. By this time, Joffre had gained a reputation as a man who favoured an offensive rather than a defensive strategy. He had weeded out senior officers in the French Army who he believed were defensively minded and replaced them with like-minded men.

Joffre was given the credit for stopping the German advance on Paris and in stemming this advance at the Battle of the Marne. However, he also became associated with the stalemate of trench warfare that occurred on the Western Front and the failure of anybody in a position of leadership to come up with a strategy to end trench warfare.

Joffre gained a reputation for not panicking in difficult situations and despite all the horrors that the French soldiers endured in the trenches and at battles like Verdun, he was nicknamed "Grandpère" by the soldiers. He did lack tactical and strategic imagination which did ensure that trench warfare continued - but other military leaders like Douglas Haig and Eric von Falkenhayn were also considered to be like this and they were all probably the products of the military schools that they attended. Their military education certainly could not have visualised the mayhem of trench warfare.

However, Joffre did lose credibility by the failure of the breakthrough at the Somme. This battle had been touted as the "final push" for Berlin but was deemed to be a failure. Whereas Verdun was seen as a French triumph in that the city did not fall, the Somme was costly in terms of lives lost and seemingly gained little. In December 1916, Joffre was promoted to Marshal of France and General Nivelle succeeded him as commander-in-chief of the French Army. In 1917, Joffre was appointed president of the Allied War Council and in the final months of the war, Joffre was involved in ceremonial duties as opposed to any strategic ones. Between 1918 and 1930, he held a number of posts at the Ministry of War. Joseph Joffre died in 1931.[9]

---

[9] *Marshal Joseph Joffre". HistoryLearningSite.co.uk. 2014. Web*

Field marshal Sir John French. 28th September 1852 – 22th May 1925.

Field marshal Sir John French was commander in chief of the British expeditionary force from 1914-1915. He had served as a cavalry commander during the Second Boer War which took place from 1899-1902. During this war he led the 1st Cavalry Brigade. He was later promoted to General and from 1907-1912 his role was Inspector General of the army. His promotion to Field Marshal took place in 1913.

With his history Military history behind him French was appointed to commander of the BEF in august 1914. It was

French that led the BEF at Mons against the advice of Kitchener and Haig who suggested a position further south, this decision led to the BEF being forced to make an almost immediate retreat in face of the German onslaught, with our ranks falling.

Despite his name, French's relationship with our French allies was rather fragile. There were two reasons for this. He had to be a subordinate ally to the French army which was more numerous and substantial that the BEF, providing support to General Joffre. The other reason being he had to maintain the independence of the BEF, and was frequently pushed into political debates that he would have preferred to stay out of. He could see that the years ahead would be difficult, the allies were always under pressure from the Germans, with at times unrealistic demands often with inadequate resources. French was also faced with demands from Joffre to help him with the French campaigns. Sir John French wanted to hold back, at least until the arrival of Kitchener's new army. His wishes were ignored and he was ordered to assist the French at all cost, this led to many losses at Neuve Chapelle, Aubers Ridge and Fesubert during 1915.

In terms of Sir John French and the Battle of Loos, his views seem rather hap hazard. He believed his armies should stand on the defensive until reinforced and agreed to the battle. Then his views changed, possibly as the situation became apparent that the Battle of Loos was becoming to look like a failure, his support for the battle shrank. With his changing views and decision to keep the XI Corps under his direct control, thus putting a strain on his already fragile command which in turn would put a strain on the 1st Army under the command of Haig, Haig felt he had no choice but to try and Push French out of command. From December 1915, Haig would be in control of the BEF. For the rest of the war French would be in command of the British home forces and travel to Dublin in 1916 to oversee the British forces to try and the Irish rebellion under control. He was made Lord Lieutenant of Ireland in 1918 and died in 1925.

Field Marshal Douglas Haig. 19th June 1861 – 29th January 1928

Field Marshall Douglas Haig is most associated with the Battle of the Somme in World War One. Douglas Haig was Britain's commander-in-chief during the Somme battle and took much criticism for the sheer loss of life in this battle.

Haig was born in 1861 in Edinburgh. Haig was born into a family of Scotch whisky distillers and unusually for Generals of his day had a university education at Oxford. He did not attain his degree due to absence from illness, but passed his exams so was eligible for service at Sandhurst. [10]

He was commissioned in the cavalry in 1885 and served both in the campaigns in the Sudan and in the Boer War in South Africa between 1899 and 1902. In the Boer War Haig served with distinction and he was swiftly promoted to the War Office. Here Haig helped to implement the military reforms of Richard Haldane.

In August 1914, when the war started, Haig was the general commanding the First Army Corps. He and his men fought at the Battle of Mons and the first Battle of Ypres. In December 1915, Haig succeeded Sir John French as commander-in-chief of the British Army in the Western Front.

Haig had little time for new military ideas. He was very much steeped in the ways that he knew – conventional tactics. In 1916, Haig put his belief in one final mighty push against the Germans to be executed in the Somme region of France. The French had been asking for some form of military assistance from the British to

---

[10] Peter Doyle, Loos 1915, Battle story pp:46

help them in their battle with the Germans at Verdun. Haig's plan was to launch an attack on the Germans that would require them to remove some of their troops from the Verdun battlefield thus relieving the French in Verdun.

The Somme led to the loss of 600,000 men on the Allies side; 400,000 were British or Commonwealth troops. When the battle had ended, they had gained ten miles of land. Haig has been criticised by some for his belief in the simple advance of infantry troops on enemy lines. With 20,000 Allied soldiers killed on Day One and 40,000 injured, some historians have claimed that Haig should have learned from these statistics and adjusted his tactics. He did not. However, the Somme attack was not just about antiquated tactics as the battle witnessed the use of the rolling artillery barrage that should have helped the Allied troops as they advanced. That it did not was more a comment on the fact that the Germans had dug in more deeply than British intelligence had bargained for and was less susceptible to artillery fire. Once the artillery firing had stopped, the British had all but signalled that the infantry was on its way.

The tank was first used on mass at the Somme but it did not receive the enthusiastic backing of Haig – though many senior cavalry officers were against the tank and Haig was not alone in his suspicion of it as a weapon.

Haig served until the end of the war. He was created an earl for his leadership in 1919. He died in 1928, but spent the last few years of his life working for ex-servicemen, though primarily those who had been disabled in the war. Haig was a leading light in the "Poppy Day Appeal" and the British Legion movement.11

General Friedrich Sixt Von Armin. 27th November 1851-30th September 1936.

Friedrich Sixt von Armin served during the Great War as an Imperial German field army commander. Upon mobilization he was in command of the IV Army Corps from Magdeburg, and later the Fourth Army. Friedrich

---

[11] *General Douglas Haig". HistoryLearningSite.co.uk. 2014. Web*

enlisted in a Guards Regiment as a Fahnenjunker in 1870. The Franco- Prussian War began shortly thereafter, with young Friedrich receiving serious wounds during the Battle for Saint-Privat. He was later awarded the Iron Cross II and quickly promoted to Lieutenant. After hostilities ceased, Sixt continued his military service in a wide variety of assignments, both as troop commander and as a general staff officer.

By 1911, Sixt von Armin had risen to corps level commander, replacing von Hindenburg as head of IV army Corps in Magdeburg. He commanded this corps until early 1917. At mobilization, his troops were attached to Kluck's First Army on the Western Front and thus saw plenty of action during the First Battle of the Marne. They also of course became bogged down in the subsequent years of trench warfare, seeing action at Arras, Loretto Heights, La Bassee, and on the Somme. For his leadership in these engagements, Sixt von Armin received the Pour le Merite. In 1917, he replaced Duke Albrecht as leader of the Fourth Army in Flanders, which he commanded until war's end. He later received the Order of the Black Eagle (der Schwarze Adler Orden) and oak leaves for his Blue Max award.

Following the Armistice, Sixt von Armin continued his military service as commander of Heeresgruppe A, which he led back to the homeland. He retired after demobilization in early 1919 and spent the remainder of his years in Magdeburg. He was often appeared as the guest of honour or keynote speaker at post-War social events. His hometown of Wetzlar made him an honorary citizen and still maintains a Sixt-von-Armin-Straße, but the barracks there which had been named in his honour were closed in

1992. During World War Two, Sixt's son Hans-Heinrich served as a Generalleutnant for Wehrmacht and was taken prisoner by the Soviets during the Battle of Stalingrad, 1942. General der Infanterie Friedrich Sixt von Armin died in Magdeburg on 30th September 1936.[12]

The overall concept for the battle had been that Joffre's two pronged attack would work and he hoped this attack would win the war. The main strike in champagne was to be an entirely French affair. There would however be some assistance from the British just north of Lens, near the town of Loos. Warning signs were seen from the very beginning. General Haig has been a character of much scrutiny because of his role in the Somme offensive however, he was no fool during 1915. He declared,

"Flat ground would be unsuitable for an attack because the flat ground would be swept with machine gun fire."[13]

Either way Haig had to act. He commanded the 1st army and his hope was to secure the line at Loos and the Hulluch road. He had further plans too takin hill 70 then advance to the Heute Deute canal, an attack involving a wide front. His main plan was to use a relatively new invention, chlorine gas. If you have ever been to a public swimming baths, you get a tiny portion of what the soldiers were exposed to 100 years ago. As you walk in to public swimming pool you can smell the chlorine, and when you jump in the water, you instinctively rub your eyes, for the soldier's 100 years ago it was much worse.

Chlorine on the chemical element table is represented with the symbol Cl. Usually it is the second lightest halogen and

---

[12] http://home.comcast.net/~jcviser/aok/sixt.htm
[13] My boy jack pp93

at this level invisible to the naked eye. As previously stated is it used in modern swimming pools, but 100 year ago the Germans found an alternative use for this chemical. They multiplied the volume enough to cause severe harm to humans and they first used it at Ypres against the British and the Indian troops fighting for Britain.

The British found out the terrible effects of this gas for a second at the Battle of Loos but used in in a counter attack against the Germans. Chlorine gas kills by irritating the lungs so much that they are flooded, the victim actually drowning in their own body fluids. Men killed by gas show startling blueness of the lips and face, a function of the blood becoming starved of oxygen.[14]

Haig was promised 50000 cylinders of gas, sufficient to cover a front of 6300 yards. Unfortunately on September 6th Haig was instructed by France to extend the front to 14,500 yards. This meant there would only be enough gas for a 24 minuets! In addition when Haig had requested some flexibility of the when the battle was to begin to see if he could set the date when the wind would be most beneficial to the BEF The reason he asked this was to make sure the Gas attack would be successful as possible. Haig's request fell on death ears and was told regardless of any conditions, be it weather or anything else, six divisions would attack the lines between the La Bassee canal and Lens on the 25th of September 1915 after a preliminary release of Gas and smoke. The gas was referred to as the accessory due to security reasons. One of those watching its first use by the British was a man called General Rawlinson.

---

[14] Loos 1915, Peter Doyle pp: 22

"I witnessed the sight from the top of a fosse some three miles from the front line and the view before me was one I shall never forget. Gradually a huge cloud of white and yellow gas rose from our trenches to a height of two and three hundred feet, and floated quietly towards the German trenches"15

Haig had noticed two other factors going against the British. The battle field was full of slag heaps and mine works and afforded the Germans excellent defensive positions.16

Even with all this knowledge the attack had to commence and began with a four day artillery bombardment.

The four day artillery bombardment prior to the attack used up 250,000 shells and was assisted by the Royal Flying Corps, however as with many cases during the Great War, the bombardment and the assistance from the Royal Flying Corps had not been as successful as hoped. The Royal Flying Corps had also carried out the first tactical air raids in history when bombing the railway lines, marshalling yards and troop trains. The release of gas was also to be a major problem, for example affecting the attackers of the 1st division when released by the 15th division. The gas drifted back to the British lines when the wind changed direction. This would have been made worse when the troops removed their gas masks as they were confident the gas attack had worked, plus the fact they were struggling to breathe through them and see through the eye lenses, which clouded up with condensation from the

---

[15] THE FIRST WORLD WAR. A MISCELLANY. Norman Ferguson. Pp:73-74.
[16] THE FIRST WORLD WAR. A MISCELLANY. Norman Ferguson. Pp: 72.

troop's breath. In addition to this confusion it was to become evident that the troops of the XI corps were not positioned anywhere close enough to support an initial breakthrough.

The battle started at 6.30 am on September 25th. First corps comprising 2nd, 7th and 9th divisions attacking to the north of IV corps, which consisted of the 1st, 15th and 47th division. The 2nd division were repulsed by strong resistance from the Germans.

The 9th Scottish division had some success and managed to take the Hohenzollern Redoubt but were soon halted by new German Reinforcements. The 47th London Division took all its objectives and the 15th Scottish division managed to capture Loos and Hill 70. This Scottish success of capturing the Hohenzollern Redoubt, the town of Loos and Hill 70 has made this first day throughout history seem a Scottish victory, it was one of very few victories during this horrendous battle.

The 7th and 1st division encountered fierce fighting near Foss 8 and were unable to reach the German second line owing to the lack of support and in the face of brutal counter attacks were withdrawn during the night of the 25th.

The day after the 21st and 24th division were cut down in No Man's Land. On the 27th the attacks on the quarries and Hill 70 failed after sporadic and fierce exchanges of Trench warfare set in. with the Dump and Hill 70 in German hands this afforded their artillery with excellent observations of the British lines these leading to heavy casualties which included several high ranking senior officers. One of the men who would go down in history as one of these fallen officers on this day was a young man called John Kipling, the son of Bombay born British author Rudyard Kipling. His death was recreated for the Television show my boy jack produced in 2007. Dr Nick Lloyd released extracts from his lecture on the Battle of Loos for the Defence Academy of the United Kingdom.17

Dr Lloyd spoke of the inaccuracies early on in his 40 minute presentation. The film showed the Irish Guards led by John Kipling, going over the Trenches at 7.30 am, no doubt chosen to reflect the famous zero hour of the Somme offensive in 1916. The men get about 40 yards before being mown down, Dr Lloyd told his audience that the attack took place at 3pm and they walked down a hill into the quarries where they were then shot at, Young john, was last seen stumbling around, his famous spectacles that before had stopped him enlisting in the army on the ground, half of johns face, hanging off his cheek. He was never seen again.

---

[17] https://www.youtube.com/watch?v=isJE8clU6hY

The fighting was generally a disaster from the 27th and the Germans recaptured the Hohenzollern Redoubt on the 3rd of October. The last day, October 13th was one of the most disastrous, but this of course is what the book is about and shall be carried on later in the other chapters. The number of Casualties was high, some 61,000 over the course of the 18 day battle, the death toll on the first day alone had been 6,300. The Loos memorial commemorates over 20,000 that have no known grave. There were many Gallant acts on during that battle but a few, were seen to be so brave that some men received the highest Honour possible, the

Victoria Cross and it is with these men who we shall now focus on.

Captain Arthur Forbes Gordon Kilby VC MC 1885-1915.

Captain Arthur Kilby served with the 2nd south Staffordshire Regiment and was killed in action on the first day of the battle whilst leading his company attacking enemy positions near Cuinchy on the Le Bassee Canal. Kilby's heroism and gallantry during this attack was noted and he was posthumously awarded the Victoria Cross on March 30th 1916.

At his own request, and because of the gallantry he had displayed at pervious battles Kilby was selected to lead his company in an attack on of the many Redoubts in the area. Although wounded from the outset he continued to lead his men right up to the enemy wire, this whilst under heavy machine gun fire and under a shower of bombs. It was at this point he was shot down, and his foot blown off, despite this he continued to cheer his men forward and was still able to use his rifle. He was not seen again, declared missing and later presumed dead. His body was found on the 19th of February 1929 and he was interned at the Arras Road Cemetery, Roclincourt, plot 11 Row N, Grave 27.

Piper Daniel Laidlaw VC 1875-1950.

Piper Daniel Laidlaw was perhaps one of the more famous characters who took part in the Battle of Loos. The Piper in the 7th Battalion of the 15th Scottish division, was awarded the Victoria Cross for most conspicuous bravery prior to an assault of German trenches near Loos and Hill 70 again on the first day of the battle like the previous VC recipient. During the worst of the bombardment, piper Laidlaw, seeing that his company were badly shaken from the effects of the gas, with absolute coolness and disregard for danger, mounted the parapet, march up and down and played the company out of the trench with his Bagpipes. The effect of this splendid example was immediate and his company sought the courage to leave their trench and dashed forward to carry out their assault. Piper Laidlaw continued playing until he was himself, wounded.

One of the benefits of a man surviving an attack is the fact he can leave an account of his actions and the London Gazette published his account on November 18th 1915.

"I at once got the pipes going and the laddies gave a cheer as they started off for the enemy lines. As soon as they showed themselves over the trench top they began to fall fast, but they never wavered, but dashed straight on as o played the old air they all knew, Blue bonnets over the border

I ran forward for all I knew, and just as were getting near the German lines I was wounded by shrapnel in the left ankle and leg. I was too excited to feel the pain just then but scrambled along as best as I could. I changed my tune to the standard on the Braes o' Mar, a grand tune for charging on!

I kept on piping and hobbling after the laddies until could go no farther, and they seeing the boys had won the position I began to get back as best as I could to our own trenches."

Daniel Laidlaw recovered from his wounds and continued to serve until 1919, by 1917 he had become a Sergeant. Laidlaw died in 1950. His story did not end there, in 2005 two pipers from the kings own Scottish borderers and a young piper Kevin Laidlaw, Daniel's own great grandson, walked from the centre of Loos-en-Gohelle to the former site of the German front line playing the patriotic tunes played by Daniel Laidlaw.

James Dalgleish Pollock VC 1890-1958

Pollock was born on June 3rd 1890 in Tillycoultry, Clackmannanshire. His Regiment was the Queen's own Cameron Highlanders and he held the Rank of Captain, but at the time was a Corporal, his actions on September 27th awarded him the Victoria Cross. On September 27th 1915, when the enemies bombers, in superior numbers, were successfully working up the Little Willie trench towards Hohenzollern redoubt, Corporal James Dalgleish Pollock, of the Queens Own Cameron Highlanders, got out of the trench, walked along the top edge with the utmost coolness and disregard of danger, and compelled the enemies bombers to retire by bombing them from above. Though under heavy machine gun fire, he held up the progress of the Germans for an hour, being at length wounded. He died aged 67 on May 10th 1958 in Ayrshire.

Sergeant Harry Wells VC 1888-1915.

Harry Wells was born on the 19th September 1888, and after leaving school became a farm labourer. It was in the years just after the Boer War that he decided to join the Army and joined the Royal Sussex Regiment, 2nd Battalion. He had left the Regiment by 1911 but remained a reservist and was serving Kent as a policeman in 1914. On the outbreak of war, he re-joined Royal Sussex Regiment, again with the 2nd Battalion. Wells fought in two major battles, such as Aisne in September 1914, the first Battle of Ypres in October 1914. As the year passed his Regiment saw heavy losses at Auber's Ridge in May 1915, and it was during this time he was promoted to Sergeant.

His next fight, at Loss would prove to be his last. The citation from the London Gazette dated November 18th 1915 tells of his final charge.

For the most conspicuous bravery near Le Routoire on the 25th of September 1915. When his platoon officer had been killed, he took command and led his men forward to within 15 yards of the German wire. Nearly half of the platoon were killed or wounded, and the remainder very much shaken, but with the utmost coolness and bravery Sergeant Wells rallied and led them forward. Finally when very few were left, he stood up and urged them forward once more, but while doing so he himself was killed. He gave a magnificent display of courage and determination.

Harry wells was buried close to where he fell but was moved in the mid-1920s to the Dud Corner cemetery, Loos.

Captain Anketell Mountray Read VC 1888-1915.

Read was actually a captain in the Royal Flying Corps but was attached to the 1st Battalion Northamptonshire Regiment when for his action at a place called Lone Tree, he was awarded the Victoria Cross. On the first day of the Battle of Loos, although suffering from the effects of Gas, Read showed conspicuous bravery going out several times to rally members of different units who were disorganised or retiring and leading them back into the firing line. He appeared utterly regardless of the danger and moved freely amongst the men until under the increasing fire he was mortally wounded.

Read had shown bravery before Loos, during operations in august 1915 and on the night of July 29th 1915 when he carried a mortally wounded officer from the action under the heavy machine gun fire and rainstorm of grenades.

The battle was to last 18 days, the death toll, could easily reach 3000 a day and on the penultimate day, October 12th the North Staffords arrived in a desperate attempt to take the Hohenzollern Redoubt on the following day. The final day was described in an article in the Evening Sentinel. The article was originally printed in the Daily Telegraph however was reprinted in the Evening Sentinel on October 23rd 1915.

"Mr Gibbs, a special correspondent of the Daily Telegraph sends a graphic account of the attack on the Hohenzollern Redoubt on Wednesday last week.

On Wednesday October 13th, as described in Sir John French's communication the following day, an attack was dealt after a bombardment and under cover of a cloud of smoke and gas to the enemy lines southwest of Hulluch to the Hohenzollern Redoubt.

We gained about a 1000 yards of trenches just south and west of Hulluch but were unable to maintain our position due to the enemies shell fire. Southwest of St Elie we captured and held the trenches behind the Vermelles Hulluch Road and the south-western edge of the quarries. The trenches on the North western area of the quarries was also taken.

Owing to the character of the battleground and the fine clear day it was possible to obtain a view of this action from the high countryside."

As with many cases the Sentinel archives are at many times illegible but the article continues to describe the gas attack and the final charge which were much easier to read and type.

"But presently, when our artillery fired there were new clouds, arising from the ground and spreading upwards in a great heavy texture. Then came our smoke. That's our gas! said a voice on one of the slag heaps, amidst a little group of observers, and the wind is dead right for it said another voice. The Germans will get a taste of it this time. Then there was silence and some of those observers held their breath as though that gas had caught their own throats and chocked them a little. They tried to pierce through that great bar of cloud to see the drama behind its curtain. Men caught in them fumes, the terror stricken flight before its advance, the sudden cry of the enemy trapped in their dug outs.

Later on from our place of observation there was one brief glimpse of human element in this scene of impersonal powers and secret forces. Across a stretch of ground beyond some of those zig zag lines of trenches little black things were seen scurrying forward, they were not bunched together in groups, but scattered. Some of them seemed to hesitate, and then seem to fall and where they fell others hurrying on until they disappeared in the drifting clouds.

It was all that one could see of our infantry, who were led by the bombers. The enemy were firing a tempest of shells, some of them were curiously coloured of pinkish blue or with orange shaped puffs of vivid green. They were poisonous shells giving out noxious gasses. All the chemistry of death was poured out on both sides. Below it and in it our men fought with fierce valour and in these fields swept by shell fire from heavy guns reached the enemy trenches and earth works. For 1000 yards they carried the German first line trenches to the south and west of Hulluch and swept up the main trench of the Hohenzollern Redoubt.

But the enemy was strong, as usual in machine guns and held some of their trenches with desperate courage while those that were captured came under the fire of their batteries. There were many acts of magnificent courage and superb endurance from the officers and men in this difficult position. Only by the most resolute valour have they held the ground which was gained at the cost of many lives."[18]

With that vivid description of the battle field, it becomes almost possible to imagine the scene of the different coloured gasses floating around, and the view of the small figures of the men from the observation posts on the slag heaps. The popular history of the Great War published in 1933 gives a simplified, even tamed down version of the day's events.

The last big event at the Battle of Loos was the fine attack made by a division of English Territorials on the lost Hohenzollern Redoubt. This was the 46th, the men from the Midlands, who on the 13th assaulted the destructive stronghold. The 4th Leicesters, 5th Lincolns, 5th North Staffords and 5th South Staffords were the attackers, and in superb fashion they reached their objective. Once there, the Staffords on the right were shot down in scores, the

---

[18] The Staffordshire sentinel, October 23rd 1915 page 6.

Lincolns and Leicesters got somewhat farther, but met almost the same fate.19

Now follows chapter two which will follow the accounts of the Staffordshire men who survived this hellish day.

---

[19] A popular history of the Great War, Volume VI, The Armistice and after PP: 424

Chapter two:

Potters forever! The final attack and various accounts of the slaughter.

"The memorable charge in which the 5th North Staffords took part in last week is graphically described in a number of letters which have reached the Sentinel office from men who participated in the attack. One cannot read these accounts without feeling a lot of pride at the heroism described by our local Regiment. Their Nobel deeds have shed an imperishable lustre upon the splendid military traditions of North Staffordshire, and should be a spur to those who have as yet hung back to fill the depleted ranks and help to win honours for our gallant and fearless Regiment."[20]

As for being a brilliant example of military recruitment propaganda, making the reader feel the need to enlist the above article also proves to be a great introduction for this chapter. It is from accounts and letters of the time and the generous contribution from Andrew Thornton of his own work that will make up the following chapter.

PREPERATIONS FOR ATTACK

The major factor that makes the final attack against the Hohenzollern Redoubt is the sheer bravery of the local men who went over the top on that fateful day. This next chapter will focus on the days running up to the attack, the final attack its self and the immediate aftermath, although this book is a study in to the North Staffordshire Regiment, it will be necessary to use accounts from other Regiments,

---

[20] The Staffordshire weekly Sentinel, October 23rd 1915.

most notably the South Staffordshire Regiment in order to get the clearest and most accurate account of the day.

The main aim was to capture the Hohenzollern Redoubt. For those new to military history the following description of the redoubt was given in the sentinel on the 99th anniversary of the attack in 2014.

"The Redoubt its self was a salient on a slope, which afforded an excellent field of fire for the German defenders towards the British lines. It was heavily fortified surrounded by barbed wire and several machine gun nests. The Redoubt was linked to the German lines by two trenches, known as big Willie and little Willie. Both deep, well-constructed trenches."21

The names of the trenches were supposedly jokes, referring to the Kaiser Wilhelm and his son. The name Hohenzollern itself references the German Royal family and the House of Hohenzollern, signifying its importance for both armies. Control of the Hohenzollern Redoubt was essential.

Interestingly the sentinel of yesteryear also gives a description of the Redoubt.

"The Hohenzollern, though simpler in its details is just a strong position. The Hohenzollern is very nearly a masterpiece in earth construction. It contained a vast number of machine gun nests set in dugout positions almost impregnable to shell fire."22

---

[21] The Staffordshire weekly Sentinel, October 13th 2014 pp:16.
[22] The evening sentinel, October 23rd 1915 pp: 6.

A rare photograph showing the inside of the Hohenzollern Redoubt.

In order to make the layout of the battle clearer this map can be used for reference.

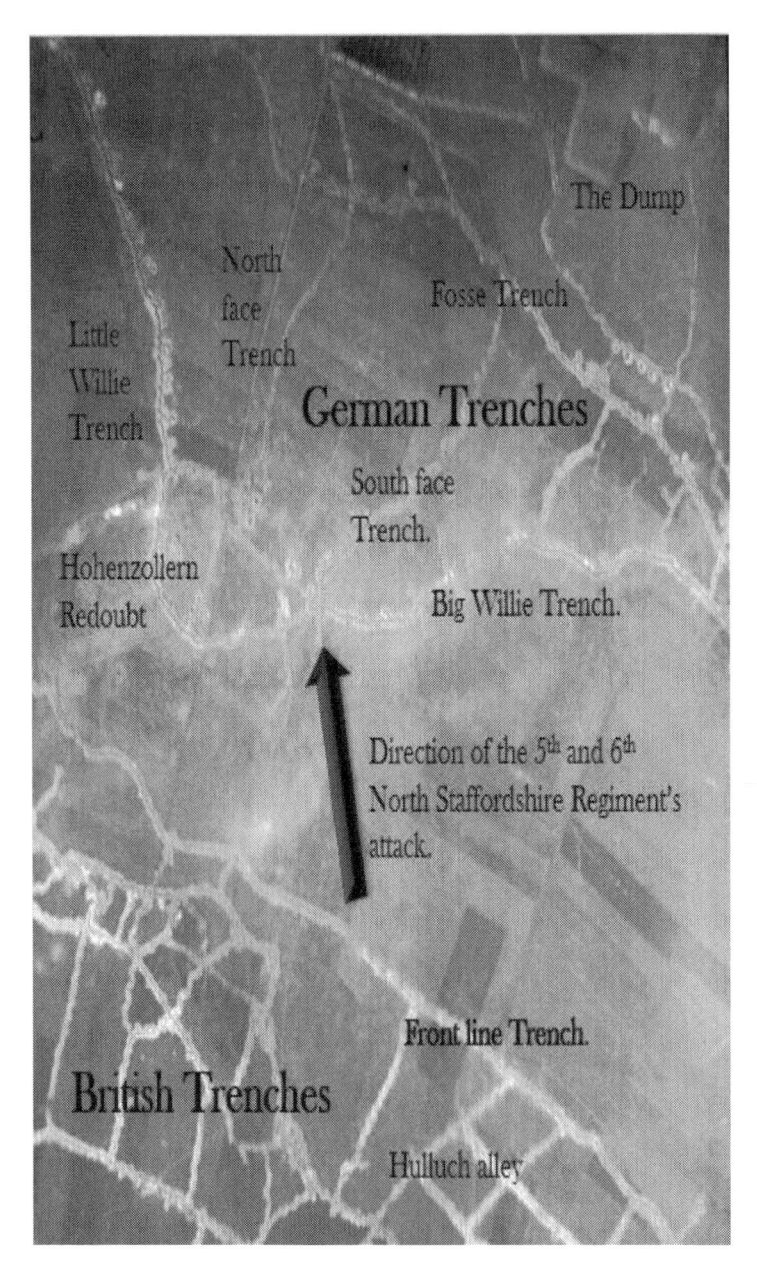

As mentioned previously The Battle of Loos commenced on 25 September 1915. In an attempt to prevent the movement of German reserves, several divisions along the front held by the British Army were ordered to make diversionary attacks, or to participate in "demonstrations". To the north of the British line, 46th (North Midland) Division, commanded by Major General E. J. Montague-Stuart-Wortley were holding the sector around Hill 60 in the Ypres Salient when the Loos Offensive began. On 25 September, the Divisional Artillery bombarded German trenches in the area while 3rd Division made an attack at Hooge. Private Sidney Richards, serving with the Machine Gun Section of the 1/5th South Stafford's, witnessed the bombardment:

"A terrible bombardment started all along our line. The Belgian battery behind us fired over 24 shells a minute. It was a fine sight watching the guns blazing away, the flashes illuminating the ruined villages in the darkness of the night."

A few days later the Division received orders to move south to participate in the Battle of Loos. Before they were relieved at Hill 60, several senior staff officers visited the units to wish them luck. Lieutenant Colonel T. F. Waterhouse, the commanding officer of the 1/6th South Stafford's, recalled in his diary what happened when his Battalion received one such visitor:

"A very senior officer of the Staff concluded his address of farewell to the Battalion with the following words, which have never been forgotten: '... And I shall watch the future career of the 6th South Stafford's with the greatest interest and sympathy. "Where's my car?"

The Division now began their journey south. The main

body of troops marched to railway stations some way behind the lines and entrained. The Transport Sections made their way towards the concentration area by road. The Staffords, together with other units, detrained at Fouquereuil, near Bethune between the 2 and 3 October in preparation for their deployment. The Division was now under the command of 11th Corps, which formed part of the 1st Army.

After a few days in billets around Robecq, the 137th (Staffordshire) Brigade moved to new areas. The 1/5th and 1/6th South Staffords were located in quarters at Vaudricourt, while the 1/5th and 1/6th North Staffords moved to billets in and around Drouvin. The Divisional Engineers; 1/1st, 1/2nd and 2/1st North Midland Field Companies, and 1/3rd North Midland Field Ambulance were located at Fouquieres, while 1/2nd and 1/3rd North Midland Field Brigades of the Royal Field Artillery moved to billets around Busnes.

Soon after their arrival in the area, senior officers from the Division attended conferences at their respective Brigade Headquarters where they were informed of the impending operation in which 46th Division were to participate.

The division's objective was to attack and capture the Hohenzollern Redoubt and the immediate area behind it. The Redoubt, located on a slight slope that afforded excellent observation and fields of fire for the Germans, was a formidable fortification. The position took the form of a salient that protruded into "No Man's Land". The Redoubt was linked to the German front line by two trenches; "Big Willie" and "Little Willie", both of which were deep, well-fortified positions that contained several machine-gun positions. "Big Willie" trench was partially occupied by the British, a trench block being the only barrier between the two sides. Two communication trenches; North Face and South Face, lead back to "Fosse" and "Dump" trenches, which were built in the shadow of a large slagheap known as the "Dump". At the base of the slagheap was a mine, "Fosse 8". The engine house of "Fosse 8", as well as the "Madagascar" cottages: the ruins of the corons, or miner's houses, were also key German defensive strong points. "No-Man's Land" was very exposed to machine gun and rifle fire from the Redoubt and the corons. The position had been captured by the 9th (Scottish) Division on the first day of the battle, but had been recaptured shortly afterwards. An attempt by 28th Division to recapture it had failed, a task now allotted to the North Midland men.

Officers from all units of the Division went to Vermelles to carry out a reconnaissance of the ground over which they were to make their attack. Having met their guides from the Guards Division who were holding the sector at this time, groups of officers from the Brigade made their way up the communication trenches to the front line. The trenches were cut into the chalky ground but had been badly damaged during the earlier fighting. The wet conditions made the trenches very slippery, a situation which was not improved by the drainage channels that had been dug in the centre of the walkway. Using trench periscopes to scan the area, the Guards directed the assembled officers' attention to the key points of the objective; the redoubt itself, the Dump, the engine house of Fosse 8 and the ruins of the corons. A group of officers from the 1/6th South Staffords made a visit to the line on 7 October, but their survey had not been completed by nightfall and the party had to go back to their billets. Their return journey coincided with one of the Guards Battalions being relieved, which made the communications trenches even more congested than usual. The following morning, the party reassembled and was driven to Vermelles on motor buses to complete the reconnaissance. On reaching the village Lieutenant-Colonel Waterhouse of the 1/6th South Staffords was severely wounded in the head when a shell burst near the party. He was evacuated to 6th Casualty Clearing Station at Lillers and required surgery on his wounds, which resulted in him losing an eye. Major "Fred" Law took over command of the Battalion.

On the afternoon of 8 October, the Germans attacked Big Willie trench. 46th Division was immediately placed on standby to move up to the line in case of a breakthrough. The troops holding the position at the time, the 3rd Grenadier Guards, were hard pressed, with two companies virtually surrounded. The 3rd Coldstream Guards launched a counter-attack and the Germans were eventually beaten back. However, a large portion of Big Willie had been taken by the Germans and would later compel the staff at 46th Division Headquarters to alter the locations of the assembly trenches from where the assault would commence.

While the plans for the assault were being formulated, the troops carried out training, including route marches and Physical Training, near their billets. New drafts of men also arrived from the Division's Base Depot in Rouen to bring the units up to strength. Among the new arrivals was Private Joseph Barlow, a soldier from Fenton, who was part of a draft of 50 men for the 1/5th North Staffords that arrived at Drouvin on 7 October. He recalled that: "On the Saturday we had lectures & c., on the coming charge." Private Sidney Richards of the 1/5th South Staffords, was billeted at Vaudricourt. He recorded his activities in his pocket diary:

7th October Bomb practice. Machine gun practice.

8th October Machine gun, bomb throwing. Night had to stand to.

9th October Machine gun practice. Bomb throwing.

10th October Machine gun practice. Bomb throwing.

Each Battalion at this time had a "platoon" of bombers, consisting of a Battalion Bombing Officer, a Sergeant and 32 other ranks. The importance of using hand grenades in the close-quarter battles that usually took place in trench warfare had increased by this point. Although several patterns of grenades were in existence at the time, the recently introduced Mills Bomb was considered to be the best weapon available. Following the Guards Division's defence of Big Willie, where it was estimated that 3rd Coldstream had used around 5,000 Mills Bombs, the bombers of 46th Division were issued and trained with this type of grenade alone. To assist the bombers in their training, they practised carrying out attacks on dummy trenches that had been constructed near Fouquieres by the Divisional Engineers.

As well as digging the practice trenches, the Royal

Engineers of 46th Division also sent sections forward into the front line to carry out repairs and improvements. Other essential work was also being carried out, as detailed in the War Diary of 1/3rd North Midland Field Ambulance:

"Fouquieres - 10.10.15

Instituted system of latrines in which the faecal matter is at once burnt in an incinerator within the latrine enclosure - urine passed into a separate receptacle + supplied into a urine bucket.

Got working the engine in an adjoining Steam Laundry. Men of the unit repairing the boiler - using the appliances facility as Baths + pantry for washing & drying clothes, Hospital Towels etc."

A model of the Hohenzollern Redoubt and the surrounding area had also been constructed in a field outside Divisional Headquarters at Gosnay. The British line was marked out with green tape, the German positions in white, with bricks and pieces of coal positioned to represent the key features. All ranks were encouraged to visit the model to familiarise themselves with the ground, as they had no opportunity of going into the front line to do so before the attack. Private S. Orpe of the 1/5th North Staffords recalled that:

"It was here that our Colonel gave an explanation of what we had to do, and was quite jolly over it."

Divisional Headquarters issued the Operation Orders on 10 October detailing the objectives for the coming assault. The original plan had been to deploy 137th Brigade in the forward line to the east of Big Willie. However, the fighting that had taken place on 8 October, as well as the complicated layout of the trenches in the locality, made this impossible. Major General Montague-Stuart-Wortley therefore decided that both of the brigades that were to carry out the attack, 137th and 138th (Lincoln and

---

[23] The evening sentinel October 30th 1915, an image of Samuel Orpe.

Leicester) Brigades, would commence their advance from the old front line from where 9th Division had made their assault on 25th September. Stuart-Wortley was also been in favour of mounting a sequential attack on the trenches around the Hohenzollern Redoubt, capturing and securing one position at a time before moving forward to take another. 11th Corps Headquarters overruled this plan and 46th Division's assault would follow basically the same pattern as that used by 9th Division. 137th Brigade was to be on the right of 46th Division's attack and were to link up with 12th (Eastern) Division, who were detailed to capture the neighbouring "Quarries" position:

"The 137th Brigade from the old British front trench between G. 10. b. 98 and G. 4. d. 26 and assembly trenches in the rear will assault at 2 p.m. with their left directed on the N.W. corner of the DUMP.

1st Objective: - Track crossing FOSSE ALLEY at G. 5. b. 68 - G. 5. b. 39 and A. 29. d. 22 to PENTAGON REDOUBT at A. 29 C. 53 (inclusive). The assault will pass straight on without pause to the far side of the DUMP. Bombing parties will be told off by the Commander, Right Attack to bomb along the following trenches as they are successfully reached by the assault.

i) SOUTH FACE.

ii) FOSSE ALLEY to join up with the left of 12th Division about the track at G. 5. b. 68.

iii) Trench running towards 3 CABARETS from A. 29. D. 22.

Bombing parties will also be organised to deal with DUMP TRENCH and SLAG ALLEY and with machine-gun emplacements and other defences found in the DUMP, and clear them of the enemy. Dug-outs must be cleared by bombing and the greatest care that none are left unsearched.

2nd Objective: - A.29.d.25 - 3 CABARETS, N.E. edge of CORONS DE PEKIN - W. edge of CORONS DE MAROC - railway A.29.c.(exclusively)."

The artillery allocated for the operation consisted of three Heavy Artillery Groups, under the control of the commander of 11th Corps, and one group of Divisional Artillery, consisting of six field brigades and one howitzer brigade, under the command of the C.R.A. of 28th Division. The 46th Division's artillery would form part of this group, but 4th North Midland Brigade, equipped with 4.5-inch Howitzers, would be placed under the control of the C.R.A. of 12th Division to support their attack. The 137th Brigade would have direct artillery support provided by 22nd Brigade, Royal Field Artillery.

The artillery would also provide detachments to assist with creating a smoke screen in front of the trenches. Five 95mm mortars and two Stokes Mortars were issued, crewed by a detachment drawn from the five units of the Divisional Artillery. Each party would consist of one Officer, a Sergeant and ten other ranks. The crews of the Stokes Mortars, one from the Divisional Ammunition Column, the other drawn from 1st North Midland Field Brigade, would provide the smoke screen in front of the infantry to allow them to form up under cover prior to making their advance. The task of the 95mm mortar teams was to provide further smoke cover for the infantry once they had reached the first objective, the intention of which was to assist with the work of consolidating the positions. The 137th Brigade was allocated the support of both Stokes Mortars and three 95mm mortars. In addition to the mortar crews, the Divisional Artillery were ordered to supply a detachment of five Officers and 250 other ranks to act as carrying parties once the assault had got under way.

The Divisional Engineers would also be committed to the operation. 1/2nd North Midland Field Company, (Major Christopher Hatton), was ordered to provide two sections that would be attached to the forward companies of 1/6th South Staffords and 1/6th North Staffords. Two sections of 1/1st North Midland Field Company, (Major Samuel Tonks), would support the 138th (Lincoln and Leicester) Brigade. The sections would form trench-blocking parties and assist in consolidating the captured ground with barbed wire entanglements. The remaining two sections from both companies would be retained in reserve. 2/1st North Midland Field Company, (Major James Selby Gardner), was placed under the command of the C.R.E. at Divisional Headquarters.

On the evening of the 10 October, Lieutenant-General R. C. B. Haking, the commander of 11th Corps, of which 46th Division formed part, addressed the officers of the Division in the courtyard of the chateau at Gosnay. In speech that was no doubt intended to reassure and encourage them, he told the assembled group that the Division's attack would be supported by the largest concentration of artillery yet made by the British Army, and to expect little resistance from the German machine gun positions around the

Hohenzollern Redoubt. He also added that, providing that the wind was in the right direction, gas would almost certainly be used in support of the attack.

On 11 October, Brigadier Feetham issued a further Operation Order, which set out the dispositions of the units of 137th Brigade for the attack. The Brigade would deploy 1/5th South Staffords, (Lieutenant-Colonel R. Richmond Rayner), and 1/5th North Staffords, (Lieutenant-Colonel John Hall Knight), in the first line of attack. The support Battalions would be the 1/6th South Staffords, (Acting Lieutenant-Colonel F. W. B. Law), and 1/6th North Staffords, (Lieutenant-Colonel Robert Ratcliff). 1/5th North Staffords would be positioned on the left of the Brigade's frontage and would advance closest to the Redoubt. 1/5th South Staffords were split into two parts; "B" and "C" Companies were to be located in an old communications trench that was linked to Big Willie, with Battalion Headquarters, "A" and "D" Companies deployed on the right of 1/5th North Staffords. Each Battalion was ordered to make available two bombing parties and an additional detachment of bombers drawn from 139th (Sherwood Foresters) Brigade was also attached to the Staffords half of the Brigade's machine-gunners - 8 gun teams - would move forward with the third wave, while the remainder would remain in the first-line trenches to provide covering fire in support of the advance. 137th Brigade's attack was also postponed for five minutes by Major-General Montague-Stuart-Wortley, and would now take place at five minutes past two. The intention of this delay was to allow the 138th Brigade to attack the West Face of the Hohenzollern Redoubt and therefore hopefully divert the attention of the defenders from 137th Brigade's assault.

On the morning of 12th October, the Staffords paraded ready to enter the battle. Each man was issued with three days' rations, 220 rounds of ammunition and three empty sandbags, the additional ammunition being carried in cotton bandoliers. The men serving with the bombing parties carried only 100 rounds of ammunition, but were to be issued with two sacks containing grenades from a supply dump closer to the front line. In addition to this, each man had two "smoke helmets" to carry. Operation orders stipulated that prior to the release of gas in the front line, all troops were to wear their "Hypo" helmets, a primitive gas mask worn over the head. Made of cotton impregnated with chemicals that reduced the effects of chlorine gas, the hood-shaped mask had a cellulose acetate window in the front to enable the soldier to see. The troops had also recently been issued with the more advanced "Phenate" smoke helmet, which was to be kept in a satchel as a spare. The men also carried their greatcoats on their back instead of packs.

The machine gun sections, under the command of Captain Charles Caddick-Adams of the 1/5th North Staffords, assembled at Verquin at 10.00 a.m. and commenced their march up to the line. By early afternoon, the machine gunners had reached Vermelles. After unloading their limber wagons, which then made the return journey back down to their transport lines, the men trudged forward towards the communication trenches, toiling with the burden of guns, tripods, ammunition and other equipment.

The remainder of the 137th Brigade marched from their billets and also formed up near Verquin at a road junction. The 1/5th South Staffords had received orders to commence their march ahead of the rest of the Brigade and were already on their way up towards the line. The order of the march was as follows:

Brigade Headquarters

1/6th South Staffords

Detachment of Bombers from 139th Brigade

1/2nd North Midland Field Company

1/5th North Staffords

1/6th North Staffords

The Brigade Band would lead the column for part of the journey. Private J. Harrison, a Burslem man serving with the 1/5th North Staffords, was a member of one of the bombing parties. He gave a description of the first stage of the march:

"At 3.15 the Colonel's whistle sounded giving the signal "Quick March". In the space of two minutes a long line of dusty-clad warriors were gliding along that French road, some singing such songs as "Bonnie Scotland" and "Tommy Atkins" & c., whilst others (some I may say went before) heard the cracking of a bullet, or the screaming of a shell, thinking deeply of what the future may foretell, and others of the dear ones at "Home Sweet Home". On, and on we marched, past collieries and villages, the people of which stood at their doors with wide-spread eyes, wishing us a jovial "bon-sohait" and "bon-soir", as each four tramped along."

---

[24] The evening sentinel, November 13th 1915, an image of J Harrison.

Major General Montague-Stuart-Wortley watched the column march past and made encouraging remarks as the men filed by. The column eventually reached a field just outside the village of Sailly Labourse, where Private Harrison and his comrades made a welcome halt:

"The shades of evening falling rapidly when we marched on to a piece of waste ground on which fires were burning and loaves and bags of food awaiting digestion, whilst others contained the following day's rations. Here we halted after a march of about six miles and not having had anything in the food line since dinner, I can assure you we anxiously awaited some 'grub'."

The Battalion cookers had accompanied the column on its march and were already brewing dixies of tea and issuing the men with a ration of bread and bacon, which was intended to eaten for supper on the following day. After a short rest, the column was ordered to fall in and continued the march up towards Vermelles. The cookers returned to the Transport Lines at Fouquieres. It was now getting dark, and as the Staffords moved closer to the front line, the sound of artillery fire was becoming more intense. The rise and fall of flares and flashes from the guns illuminated the horizon in front of them.

Each Battalion had been ordered to provide an advance party of one Officer and ten other ranks to move forward to the Brewery at Vermelles, where the Division's Royal Engineers had established their supply park. Their task was to assist with the issuing of trench stores and equipment for the assault troops to carry up into the line. Private S. Orpe was a member of the advance party sent forward by 1/5th North Staffords:

"We set off about noon and went to Vermelles as an advance party. There we got all the tools ready for the company when they came at night. Here as we were waiting they began to shell the village. It was a good thing the troops were not coming, as they would have had it hot. Our company arrived at 8 o'clock."

Captain W. W. C. Weetman was serving with the 1/8th Sherwood Foresters. His Battalion, together with the rest of 139th Brigade, was in reserve for the attack. He recalled his impressions of the Staffordshire Territorials as they marched past him:

"We had a very pleasant and easy march up to Vermelles, where a halt was made for tea. Here we passed one of the Stafford Battalions who were to make the assault. It was too dark to see their faces, but their voices were full of confidence and cheeriness which did one good to hear."

After a brief rest at Vermelles, the Staffords marched up the road for about a mile until they reached the beginning of the communication trenches. Guides from the Divisional Cyclist Company were waiting at the entrance of Gordon Alley to lead them forward to the assembly trenches.

The 1/3rd North Midland Field Ambulance (Lieutenant-Colonel H. H. C. Dent) had received instructions to move up to the Chateau at Vermelles to act as the Main Dressing Station for 46th Division. Forty stretcher-bearers were sent by the unit to the reserve trenches to set up a Collecting Station in a communications trench, Barts Alley, to which all wounded were to be taken. From here, the stretcher cases would be taken to the Main Dressing Station, and from there would be evacuated by Motor Ambulance to one of the many Casualty Clearing Stations located behind the lines.

Two sections each from the 1/1st and 1/2nd North Midland Field Companies had already moved forward into the front line, in preparation for the arrival of the main body of the Division. Dumps of supplies: ammunition, grenades, barbed wire and tools, were already established to the rear of the front line. Further depots were placed in the communication trenches. Signboards were also erected. During the night, parties of Royal Engineers went over the parapet of the British front line to cut gaps in the barbed wire through which the infantry could advance. While carrying out work in the trenches to be occupied by 138th Brigade, the 1/1st North Midland Field Company had four men killed and one wounded when their dugout received a direct hit.

The journey up into the firing line was torturously slow, the Battalions being forced to halt several times as they struggled up the congested trenches to relieve the Guards Division. The 1/5th South Staffords had arrived at the entrance of the communication trenches before the main body of the Brigade. An anonymous Sergeant from Walsall recalled the journey in a letter home:

"As we passed through a village the Germans started to shell one of our batteries. Some of them came dangerously close to us. A little later we went across open country, and from there it took us four hours to get into the first-line trench, as there were all sorts of obstacles. The delay was largely caused by what we call "whizz-bangs", which the Germans sent over in good supply. Our first-line trench was originally the second-line German trench. All night long there were shell noses flying about, but only one man was hit, and his injuries were merely bruises."

It had been dark for several hours by the time the 1/5th North Staffords started their passage up the communication trenches. For recent arrivals at the front, such as Private

Joseph Barlow, the experience was an inauspicious introduction to the war:

"What a night! first night in the trenches too! It took us all night creeping and dodging down the different communication trenches with the "whiz-bangs" and "Jack Johnsons" bursting all around us."

It would take the Staffords until the morning of the 13 October to reach the assembly trenches and to take over responsibility for the line from the Guards. It was estimated that the distance between the entrances of the communication trenches to the assembly trenches was about one mile.

After a tiring march to their assembly trenches, the troops of 137th (Staffordshire) Brigade snatched a brief sleep before the usual "stand-to" at dawn on 13 October.

Private Harrison of the 1/5th North Staffords had reached the front line just before dawn:

"When posted to my particular bay I partook of a short but sound sleep until about 6 a.m., and at this juncture I awoke and viewed the piece of ground over which we were to charge. At 8 a.m. on that notable morning I enjoyed my last meal previous to the battle - a tin of meat and vegetables. You may guess I did justice to same."

The assembly trenches were now crowded with troops. Strict orders to keep out of sight of the Germans were adhered to. There were no dugouts in which the men could shelter, and the trenches themselves had been badly damaged during the earlier fighting. Private C. C. Oram, a soldier from Lichfield serving with "C" Company of the 1/6th North Staffords, wrote about the conditions in his section of the line:

"It was a beastly old trench, dead bodies lying about and all knocked about, having been a few days ago a German trench."

Men from 187th Special Company, Royal Engineers had also arrived in the front line trenches. This was a specialist unit formed to conduct chemical warfare, and would be providing the gas attack to support 46th Division's assault. The Company had been formed at St Omer in July 1915 and was comprised of men who had knowledge of chemistry, many of whom were university graduates. The sappers began to bring up the cylinders of chlorine gas up to the forward positions from where they would release their cargo. To allow the engineers to set up the equipment, and also to limit casualties should a cylinder burst, some of the troops in the front line were temporarily withdrawn to the reserve trenches. The sappers wore armbands made up of vertical strips of red, white and green cloth, to denote their specialist role. The direction of the wind was also noted, a gentle breeze blowing from the south-west, and was closely monitored prior to the scheduled time for commencing the gas attack.

Preparations for the artillery bombardment were also well in hand. The two companies of the 1/5th South Staffords located in the most forward position held by the Brigade were ordered to withdraw to positions in the old British front line. At mid-day, the barrage commenced. The shelling of the German line was awe-inspiring to the Staffords waiting for the assault, as Private Barlow of the 1/5th North Staffords recalled:

"Well, I cannot attempt to describe what it was like; it was acknowledged to be the fiercest bombardment the world had ever seen. I had many a look over the parapet and what a sight! For miles you could see their first line of trenches - one blazing, raging mass of flames, smoke and dust."

However impressive the bombardment may have been to Private Barlow, the artillery barrage was not effective. Although the key positions in front of 137th Brigade: South Face, Big Willie and Dump Trench came under a heavy onslaught, the machine gun emplacements located there, as well as the fortified ruins of the buildings around the Dump, were not destroyed. Half an hour into the British bombardment, the German artillery began a counter-barrage and shelled the reserve and communication trenches in the Brigade's sector. Lieutenant "Pip-Jock" Slater, the Signal Officer of the 1/6th South Staffords, recalled an incident that happened at his Battalion headquarters:

LIEUT. P. J. SLATER
(Wounded)

"We had a little mouth-organ concert while we were waiting to "go over", and had quite a merry time, though in the middle of the bombardment our telephonist got hit on the head right in the middle of us. I don't think he was badly hurt. We, Law, Lewis, Collison and myself, were all crowded into a little rabbit-hole place, and the piece suddenly buzzed in."

The British artillery continued with their bombardment. At 1.00 p.m. the mortar detachments drawn from the Divisional Artillery started to fire smoke rounds in front of the forward trenches. The sappers of 187th Special Company also began to unleash the gas. The infantry in the trenches pulled their gas masks down over their heads and tucked them into the collar of their tunics. The chlorine gas was discharged from the cylinders and smoke candles ignited by the Royal Engineers. The yellowish-green cloud began to rise and drift towards the German lines. However, despite favourable winds, the gas settled in the remains of trenches and shell holes that bisected the shattered ground. A few of the gas cylinders had also been hit during the counter-barrage, with the Brigade suffering a few gas-related casualties. The gas had also served as a warning to the German garrison in the area that an attack on them was imminent.

Despite the Corps commander's reassurances to the contrary at Gosnay three days before, machine-gun fire from the German lines raked the parapet of the British trenches, as commented on by Major Law, the acting commanding officer of 1/6th South Staffords:

"At 1.30 p.m. I heard the enemy machine guns ranging on these same trenches for five minutes. This I reported to Brigade Hqrs., saying that I believed the fire came from the direction of the 'Dump". At 1.45 p.m. they started again. I reported this, saying that more machine guns seemed to be firing, and that their fire came from the South Face trench, and rear of it."

Lieutenant-Colonel Raymer of the 1/5th South Staffords recorded that three trench periscopes were hit by machine-gun fire in his Battalion's trenches in the minutes before the attack was due to commence. It became evident to the men waiting to attack that the bombardment had failed to suppress the German machine guns, as Private Barlow observed:

"We thought that there wouldn't be a German left alive. But would you believe it, about five minutes before we charged they opened up a murderous machine-gun fire, simply sweeping our parapets. It was a mystery to us, but we still knew we had to face it in a few minutes".

As "zero hour" crept ever closer, the officers went along the assembly trenches to check that their men were ready, as well as to give them encouragement. Scaling ladders were placed against the sandbagged walls of the trench. Bayonets were fixed. Nervous eyes looked at their watches, counting down the minutes and seconds until the officers blew their whistles to signal the troops to climb over the parapet. The Staffords were ready to attack.

The view overlooking the flat battlefield looking towards the Hohenzollern Redoubt on October 13th 1915. Shells exploding, the gas and smoke can all be seen pummelling the German lines.

THE ATTACK

Large sections of the following, will be the words from the men who were there on the day, it feels appropriate that the survivors posthumously tell their story. At 2.00 p.m., the leading Battalions of 138th Brigade began their assault on the West Face of the Hohenzollern Redoubt. 2483 Private Samuel Orpe, who served with No. 10 Platoon, "C" Company of the 1/5th North Staffords, looked up over the parapet of "C" Company's assembly trench to watch their attack go in:

"As we looked over, men could be seen running across. These were the Lincolnshire's and Leicestershire's, as they charged first."

At the same time, the bombing parties, together with the first wave of assault infantry from the 1/5th North Staffords; "A" Company, (Lieutenant (Acting Captain) Guy Worthington) on the left of the Battalion frontage and "B" Company (Captain Reginald Johnson) on the right, scaled the trench ladders and climbed over the parapet. The men then moved through the pre-prepared gaps in the barbed wire in front of the trenches and out into "No Man's Land", where the officers ordered the men to lie down. The lead companies were then organised into extended order under the cover provided by the smoke screen, all the time under heavy machine-gun fire.

At 2.05 p.m., the order to advance was given. 3807 Private Tom Whitehouse, a soldier from Newcastle serving in "D" Company, recounted later how men of the Battalion shouted "Potters For Ever!" as they scrambled up to begin the attack.

"As the first wave of the 1/5th North Staffords began to move forward, a hail of machine gun and rifle fire scythed through the ranks. Captain Worthington was hit in the thigh and later found that the copy of the New Testament he was carrying in the left breast pocket of his tunic had a bullet pass through it lengthwise and was fortunate to suffer no further injury. Worthington picked himself up from the ground and continued to carry on forward, but could only see a handful of men from his company. The small group ran towards a communication trench and jumped over it, before again lying down on the other side. No other troops could be seen in the vicinity, so they raced forward to another trench and jumped down into it. This proved to be a communication trench that had been dug by 9th Division during their brief occupation of the Hohenzollern Redoubt. Captain Worthington also found several men from the South and North Staffords bombing parties, who were engaged in the attack on Big Willie, with which the trench was connected. One witness described seeing Captain Johnson standing on the parapet of the trench, waving his cane shouting, "Come on, "B" Company!" to encourage his men as they struggled over. He was wounded a few moments later, but was not seen alive again. Captain Sidney Wood, "B" Company's second-in-command, managed to reach the shelter of a shell-hole with another soldier and stayed out in "No-Man's Land" until they were able to return to their assembly trenches later that night. Lieutenant-Colonel John Knight also climbed out of the trench with his men to lead them into their first attack. He was last seen falling after being hit in his side by a bullet."

The second wave; "C" Company, (Lieutenant (Acting Captain) Charles Keary), and "D" Company, (Captain Harry Ridgway), followed the initial assault after a few moments. It was now Private Barlow's turn to climb from his trench, this will be his entire story as it is one of the most vivid accounts of the attack we have to hand.

Pte. JOS. BARLOW,
Wounded. [25]

"Just a few lines! Ones hoping they told you I'm in the best of health. Just a week ago I wrote and told you to keep your eyes open and that would be proud of the lads from the Potteries. Well I suppose you have seen the papers now and the accounts of the Battle of Loos on Wednesday in which the gallant lads of the 5th north took part.

I have read accounts of all kinds of bravery both past and present, and seen all kinds of war pictures, but as true as I live, nothing to compare with the charge on Wednesday. In a few words it was hell! Hell let loose with all its fury.

I shall begin the story properly. I will explain that 50 of us went from Rouen on Thursday the 7th and joined the Battalion at a village. On the Saturday we had lectures on

---

[25] The evening sentinel November 20th 1915, an image of Joseph Barlow proudly holding his rifle

the oncoming charge. On Tuesday afternoon, the brigade band gave us some tunes and at night they played us off to the trenches. What a night! My first time in the trenches too! It took us all night creeping and dodging down the bombardments on the trenches. Whiz bangs and Jack Johnsons bursting all around us! We never had a wink of sleep.

At 12 o'clock we started our bombardment. Well, I cannot attempt to describe what it was like. It had to be the fiercest bombardment the world had ever seen. I had a look over the parapet and what a sight! For miles one could see their frontline of trenches. One blazing, a raging mass of flames, smoke and dust. We thought there would not be a German left alive. But would you believe it about five minutes before the charge took place they opened up a murderous machine gun fire sweeping our parapets. It was a mystery to us but we knew we had to face it in a few minutes.

Just then the officers sent word along the trenches that we must set up and that they were proud of us and bid us a farewell. We blasted a cheer and sent word back we were proud of them and would follow them anywhere.

Watches were set, two o'clock, five more minuets too go. Our sleepness began to shake off. We felt at the bayonets and put our smoke helmets on. Lads were looking over the parapets at the events, regardless of the flying bullets. I shall never forget one lad, his life extinguished.

Four minutes to go- three-two, God help us – one! Up lads and at em! Up we scrambled, bullets whizzing past our ears like hailstones. Off we started. The lad on my left fell in a heap without a murmur. About five more paces, the lad on my right dropped. Then they dropped all around me in twos and threes. I wondered when my turn would come and what it would feel like. I had not long to wait. I had gone about 50 yards when BANG, CRACK! Got hit in the leg. Just throwing my arms up in the air- BANG! Copped it again in the right. Down I go.

Well that was about seven minutes past two, there I lay face downwards, wondering what would happen next. A few yards away lay seven of eight dead pals. Some dead some dying, some delirious. I felt sorrier for them than I did myself. I could not help crying and praying for the Lord to help them. You should have seen me digging a hole with my chin in the soft ground. I could not get low enough. The bullets were flying over my head with in an inch at times.

Believe me. It was just like the very earth had gone mad and Hell turned lose. You can never imagine what it was like. There I was bullets whistling over my head, the big guns roaring away shells from our guns and the Germans. The Germans screaming one over every few seconds, the German shell bursting just a few yards away from me. You can't imagine what a terrible affair a bursting shell is unless you see one.

    After dark I thought I would risk my neck and try to get back to our trenches. I unbuckled my belt and gradually took all my equipment off and crawled on my stomach acting dead when their flare lights went up. Got to our barbed wire got up and ran the other 10 yards, like a march hare and plunged head first into the trenches, wounds or no wounds. Then I started off as well as I could hobble, stumbling and striding over the dead and dying. Men who were killed in our trenches with their shells before our charge"26

What were these shells that Pirate Barlow was describing? They were the 25cm short range trench mortar called the Minenwerfer (mine launcher) and were used by the Imperial German army throughout the duration of the Great War. They were known to the British troops as Minnies. A good friend of mine, Jonathan Honeysett MBE kindly allowed me to use some of his information on the Minenwerfer after he gave an excellent presentation on the weapon at the Christmas meeting of the Newcastle under Lyme branch of the Western Front association.

FIRST WORLD WAR GERMAN ARTILLERY

THE MINENWERFER

The weapons.

The development of this weapon was commenced by German Army engineers in the 20th Century's first decade to overcome the problem of destroying defensive structures such as forts, bunkers, trenches, and barbed-wired positions, and troops within them, in static warfare.

Standard high, and medium velocity artillery shellfire, though accurate, hit their targets at a relatively 'flat' trajectory – what was needed was a cheap, short-range but easily-moved weapon that fired its projectile high into the air, dropping near vertically onto targets, where the blast would spread horizontally with maximum impact.

---

[26] The Staffordshire evening sentinel, October 23rd 1915, pp:6

The German Army eventually selected three types of "Minenwerfer" (mine-thrower) – the LMW 7.58 cm. (light mine launcher); the mMW 7.7 cm. (medium mine launcher), and the sMW 25 cm. (heavy mine launcher) that caused such havoc on the Allies' Western Front from 1915 onwards.

An even larger Minenwerfer, the 38 cm. was developed, but its weight led to difficulties manoeuvring it in cramped spaces, with no obvious advantages over the 25 cm. weapon.

The Western Front – mobile to static warfare, August to November 1914.

The rapid 150-mile advance of the invading 1st and 2nd German Armies across Belgium and Northern France, adhering to the von Schlieffen Plan in 1914, pushed the small BEF (British Expeditionary Force) and the French 6th Army back to the River Marne, the exhausted German infantry reliant on conventional mobile light and medium artillery (e.g. the 77 mm field-gun) to destroy temporary points of resistance with high-explosive shells, or air-burst shrapnel to maim allied infantry and cavalry.

Just 30 miles from Paris, the Germans suddenly deployed to their left along the River Marne, under the illusion that the BEF might exploit a gap between their 1st and 2nd Armies, so the French 6th Army rapidly counter-attacked, forcing the Germans back to the Aisne. There, they consolidated their positions along what was to become the Western Front.

While the French and British moved parallel back into Northern France and Flanders, holding the northernmost point, Ypres, by November 1914.

Static (or trench) warfare November 1914, to March 1918.

Static defence positions, some substantial, some little more than muddy ditches, and dominated by artillery superiority over infantry deployment, were gradually established along the 450-mile Western Front, following the failure of two large battles in 1914 /1915 by the German 4th Army to push the Allies out of Ypres, and offensives by British-French forces in Northern France in 1915 e.g. Neuve Chappelle and Loos.

'Quiet sectors' of the Front enabled both the Allies and Germans to build substantial systems of bunkers and fortifications, German positions often better constructed, with shell-proof reinforced concrete, and very deep, electrically lit where possible, as witnessed on the Hindenburg Line.

The 1916 French defence at Verdun, the 1916 Allied Somme offensive and the 1917 British offensive at Passchendaele, technically 'victories', cost two million casualties, as both sides sought to suppress strong-points and 'breakthrough'. Even the advent of tanks failed to achieve a decisive 'break-out' for the British at Cambrai, once German light field-gun crews realised that their high-velocity shells could penetrate armour.

Minenwerfers in action, 1915-1918.

The first generally-recorded use of Minewerfers, and in particular the large 25 cm. version, was at Loos in March 1915, where their impact was critical in enabling the Germans to maintain their line of defence – huge craters resulted in their hitting trench positions, and unnerving allied soldiers. Where trench conditions allowed the Germans to establish a Minenwerfer position, with their seven-man crew, they were increasingly deployed throughout necessary sectors, including the Somme in 1916.

Production of all three Minenwerfer types increased–1,234 heavy 25 cm. 2,361 medium 7.7 cm., and 12, 329 light 7.58 cm. weapons had been built by 1918. Their effectiveness in Eastern Front offensives, in coordination with 'Bruckmuller' selected–target artillery barrages, and fast-moving platoons from Storm-trooper companies, proven at Riga, Latvia in 1917, before the Russian Army collapse to Bolshevik revolution, ensured that ten companies in every German Battalion, had ten Minenwerfer units assigned to them. The 25 cm. Minenwerfers and their crews were one of the many reasons for initial German army success in their 1918 Spring Offensives – Operation Michael on 21st March in Northern France, and Operation Georgette on 9th April in Flanders – trench warfare was dead.

Descriptions of Minenwerfer effects on Allied soldiers in the Western Front locations that they occupied are many, and various. The first is abstracted from Denis Winter's Death's Men, Page 114:-

....The chief drawback of the mortar was that the enemy's version seemed more potent. Certainly it was larger in calibre.* The German projectile was the size of a two-gallon oil drum, loaded with 200 lb. of a wet, yellow paste, which smelt like marzipan and burst with a force that sent a wave through the soil for a mile, as if the soil had been water.

The range was over 1,000 yards, and the crews were itinerant specialists. A typical mortar shoot from the enemy line would lay down one missile per ten yards at three-minute intervals. Sharp ears were needed for the whistles from the German line, which indicated firing preparedness. Then the canister would come, turning over and over in the air and making a 'woof, woof' sound. The leisurely descent was demoralizing, as observers shouted out their warnings and men made rapid dashes for safety before the final swerve to the right and a crater the size of a large living-room at the end of it.

Cooper echoed the feelings of most front-line men when he wrote that he never got used to mortars. 'I don't know why I'm shaking. I just can't help it'. Gillespie's mind went back to school cricket fields when he recalled fielding deep and waiting for skyers. Even when swallows swooped over the trench, he would duck, calling the reflex 'sausage-eye', and involuntarily seeing his past life rising before him with every enemy shoot. Though there were a dozen bombardments for every mortar shoot, it was the feeling of exactness combined with the huge amount of explosive in every canister which triggered the fear. On one hand was the sensation of a cat playing with a mouse; on the other, vivid images of bodies bursting and disintegrating. ...* The British mortar rounds were tiny by comparison – 2 or 3 inch.

The next description is from Neil Hanson's Priestley's Wars, Page 63, in which the famous author and broadcaster, J. B. Priestley (1894-1984), a soldier in the Duke of Wellington's West Riding Regiment, recalled his diary entry for 13th March 1916:-

….Up in the line, what we did mind, what soon began to get us down, were the Minenwerfers, the big trench mortars; and at Souchez we always appeared to have the Minenwerfer specialists against us. Often we asked for their attention; not us the ordinary infantry who had to stay in the front line, but the Brigade, the Division, the Corps, and the Army.

What happened all too often was that our own specialists would rush their Stokes guns up into the support trenches, blast away for a quarter of an hour, and then

Hurry off with their infernal things to where the transport was waiting. Pampered and heartless fellows – this is how we regarded them – lunatic experts who had to interfere; off they went to some back area, to roofs and beds and estaminets, beer and wine, chips and eggs, while we poor devils, left behind in holes in the ground, now had to face the anger of the Boches they had been strafing.

The Minenwerfer teams got to work on us. Up and then down came those monstrous canisters of high explosive, making hell's own din when they landed, blasting or burying us. If there was any infantryman who was not afraid of these things, who was not made uneasy by any rumours they would be shortly arriving, I never met him. Perhaps because they were such short-range affairs, perhaps because if you were on the alert, looking and listening hard, you could just dodge them, perhaps because they made such a hellish row, they frightened us more than bullets, bombs, and shells of all calibres. And in and around Souchez we crouched below a nest of them. ….

On Page 68, Priestly describes how his luck ran out in early June 1916. A Minenwerfer shell landed on his position and buried him alive as the trench collapsed. His comrades dug him out, and he was sent back to 'Blighty' to recover, where following convalescence, he returned to the Western Front with a commission in 1918, and was de-mobbed in 1919.

The final descriptions of Minenwerfers in action were translated from the Flemish book – 80 Jaar Slag oom de Kemmelberg – and the accounts of a French Army officer at the Battle of the Lys in April 1918 (the German Operation Georgette). The 39th French Infantry Division lost over 5,000 men on Mt. Kemmel as they fought the German 56th Division who had seized the summit on the 25th April – their observers saw sun glinting on the Channel waters. This French division relieved my father's surviving 1st/9th Royal Irish Fusiliers 'composite Battalion'* – just 400 men from 2,600 – on the 19th April. The French officer writes:-

"….29th April 1918: Destruction of the Castle of Loker

On the 27th and 28th of April the Germans recommenced their strategy of mass attack. Their artillery shelled the French positions without halt using every type of shell size available. The German Minenwerfers (mine throwers) 250 mm. artillery crews came into action and created a great deal of destruction. The "M.W. 250" was a weapon of great repute. It was easy to move around, and its calibre remained impressive for a small artillery piece. ……"

Jon Honeysett MBE, BA (Mod. &.Int.Hist.)

* Blacker's Boy's ISBN 978-0-9572695-0-7. History of the 9th Battalion, Royal Irish Fusiliers 1914-1919.

When a British soldier referred to a whiz bang, it was this weapon he was describing, because that's what it did, fell down with a sharp whistle and then exploded with a horrifying bang and would leave a crater around the same size of an average living room. The 25cm Minnie, was easily transportable and could be carried and quickly assembled by just four men, or transported intact, when put on a cart and pulled by a horse. The shell stood at 3ft 6 inches tall, was packed with 250 pounds of explosives, but what made this weapon even more deadly was it was packed with shards of scrap metal. It could easily destroy trenches and tear men to shreds. As Jon's article already stated the weapon had been documented that when it exploded there was a smell similar to that of Marzipan, and a direct hit would turn a man into a grey mass, leaving hardly anything left that would identify the person as a person. In some cases the family may retrieve his army tag if that was stored away under his tunic, and that would be the only thing they would have to remember him by.

Although not of a man of the North Staffordshire Regiment, Captain Sidney Rogerson, 2nd West Yorkshire Regiment, 23rd Brigade gives a detailed account of the effects of a Minenwerfer.

"Standing over 3 feet 6 inches in height and filled with nearly two hundred pounds of high explosive , they had a more demoralising effect than any other single form of enemy action. There was no sound of distant discharge to give warning of their coming. Ears had to be sharp indeed to hear the warning whistle blown by the German gunners before they fired their mortars. Eyes had to be fixed in the air to watch for the shape which would soar ponderously upward, turn slowly over and over in its downward flight....and with a woof! woof! woof! Burst with a shattering crash, sending long jagged strips of metal whirring savagely for yards and rendering into fragments everything around. The very leisureliness of their descent was demoralising. The immense clamour of their explosion was demoralising. But most demoralising was the damage they could do. Men do not easily or soon throw off the shock of seeing all that could be found of four of their comrades carried down for burial in one ground sheet."27

The power of this weapon was immense, and this is a major reason there are hardly any graves of men from the North Staffordshire Regiment. There was simply nothing left of many of them. Initially it was the machine gun fire that killed and injured the men, however the Germans would fire the Minnies to clear the battle ground of any survivors and to stop the advance of anymore men, if such an attack was planned. There are not many men who survived a bombardment from this devastating weapon, so that makes Private Barlow's account unique.

---

[27] http://www.pollingerltd.com/bookshop/martin_body/2nd-devons-minenwerfer.pdf

A Minenwerfer captured by the Canadian army near Vimy Ridge in April 1917. This was donated to the newly set up imperial war museum and became one of the museums first major exhibits, it is now currently housed in the imperial war museum North in Manchester.

Now, let's get back to the main attack and more accounts of the slaughter. Private Orpe advanced with his comrades of "C" Company:

"Then came the words; "Over, Staffords!" There were cheers and smiles, only to change to death and pain, men falling everywhere. It was an awful sight, as it was but one mass of dead and wounded. I got about 40 yards across when I got hit in the foot. As the bullets were hitting the ground where I lay, I kept still for a while. I then began to crawl into a trench in front of me."

2457 Private Arthur Preston, who came from Stone, was a member of "D" Company:

"When our Company got over, the first thing that met our eyes was the chaps lying in front, some dead and others wounded. It took me all my time to keep in touch with them, as they were mowing us down so fast with machine guns. I was just thinking to myself what Frank asked me for, when a bullet struck me in the calf of my left leg. I lay down and rooted myself in for safety and got my puttees off. I dressed the wound with my field dressing, and then I crawled back to our trench, which was full of dead and wounded who had been fetched in."

The advance of the second wave suffered the same fate as the first. The remnants of the two companies had reached no further than the communication trench. Both of the company commanders had become casualties, Captain Ridgway being killed and Lieutenant Keary wounded. With their officers killed or wounded, the leaderless survivors of "C" Company linked up with the remnants of "A" Company in the communication trench and advanced no further. Captain Ridgway was mortally wounded during the advance. His servant, 2459 Private William Fielding from Stoke, went to the aid of his officer. Using his entrenching tool and under fire, he managed to scrape a hole to shelter Ridgway from any further injury. Fielding, after giving his officer a drink, then crawled back to the assembly trenches to bring a stretcher party to the aid of Captain Ridgway. Harry Ridgway was brought back to the trenches but despite the efforts of Private Fielding, he died of his injuries.

On assessing the situation and the state of the men after the harrowing ordeal of crossing to the position, Major Charles Barke, the most senior officer who had survived the attempted advance, decided that the remnants of the 1/5th North Staffords would stand fast in the communication trench and make no further attempts to advance.

Private R Holden of the 1/6th Battalion of the North Staffordshire Regiment wrote a letter to his father, a Mr H Holden of Blackpool road in Burton on Trent.

"At one particular place, a line of trenches, a row of houses and some land had been taken. We arrived at the trenches which had only been taken a few days before. We waited until two o'clock in the afternoon, which had been the appointed time for the charges. An awful bombardment began at 12 noon which resulted in lots of chaps being wounded before the charge had started. At five minutes past two, we mounted the parapets, some mad, some with a thirst for German blood.

Then I witnessed the most awful sight I ever saw in all my life. Hundreds fell before we reached the German lines. I cannot describe to you what I saw, I was too excited! Later we got reinforcements as almost all our officers had been killed or wounded. I got back to our own trench, then my time came. The trench was full of fellows, dead or wounded and amidst all this I heard the cry of stretcher bearer. I wondered off to where the cry came from. Eventually I found the chap who had been hit by a shell and was lying helpless exposed to the Germans who were firing like mad. I had been spared up to then and without hesitating I jumped over the parapet and before I fell, I was shot in the thick part of my right leg. I was convinced to crawl back to our own trench as the pain was to awful.

We are the only two left out of our company, the bomb throwers, we are to thank god for his kindness. Two or three hundred of were taken out at night (to the hospital) and on the 15th I was operated on and the bullet extracted"28

Another account of the attack came from a Sergeant H Dyer in a letter to his parents, Dyer was also in the 6th Battalion.

"I have had my first experience of trench warfare, and as luck would have it I just managed to get in for a hot time. We made a magnificent charge, and only lost 16 of our platoon but what sad times there will be! My word, it was awful. Colonel Ratcliff went over and led us. Thank god he has come through all this. It was very hard for us chaps first time in!

We went to the trenches Tuesday night and made the charge at exactly 2pm on Wednesday afternoon. My word, the courage, pluck and endurance of our fellows was great. We went over the parapet like a dog after a rabbit! Didn't we give them stick, I can account for a few. We got too their trench and routed them out with bayonets and bombs. You should see the cowards holding up their hands for mercy. They say oh mercy comrade!

My senior sergeant got killed as soon as we went over the top. We held the trench for about four hours until we got supports up. Thank god I have come through without a scratch. The Grenadier Guards relived us the next morning. We are some miles back from the firing line enjoying ourselves on a big farm. The people here are very nice and will give us anything we want.

---

[28] The Staffordshire evening sentinel, 23rd October 1915. Pp:6

The horrors of the charge though, to see poor fellows fall and the wounded. It makes one have all the more spite against the German Huns."29

Dyer and his platoon although the lost men were one of the luckier groups of men during the attack and were only of only a handful to carry out their objectives successfully. The next account describe the true horrors of failure at Hohenzollern.

Private N. HYSLOP.

In a letter to his parents, back home in Newcastle under Lyme, private N Hyslop wrote this account of the attack.

"We were in the charge last Wednesday, and I was shot through the thigh just above the knee but luckily the bullet

---

[29] The Staffordshire evening sentinel, 23rd October 1915 pp:6

passed through without touching the bone, so there is nothing to fear.

We went into the trenches on Tuesday night and made the charge at two o'clock on Wednesday afternoon. I was with a party of bomber throwers and had to get over the parapet at ten past two. I advanced about 60 yards and dropped to rest, when a poor chap close by who had had his leg broken by a shot asked me to get him a stretcher bearer. As I was getting back into the trench a bullet came straight across the top of the parapet and through my leg. A chap in the trench bandaged me up and I made the best of my way out"

He then describes his time in hospital and his time in England and concluded with

"I believe the Battalion was cut up something fearful, it seemed wicked to go on. The shells, machine guns and rifles were blazing away as we went across. I think I am one of the lucky ones getting off so lightly."[30]

---

[30] The Staffordshire evening sentinel, October 23rd 1915 pp 6.

Private J Harrison.

Another account, which goes in-depth about the run up to the attack and the attack came from Burslem born private J Harrison. The letter was written to his father back home in Burslem just two days after the attack. Some of Harrison's accounts have already been included, to give a chronological account, but what follows is the entire account.

"I will now relate to you how I did my duty in a most horrible charge on Wednesday last and how I came out of the farce with only a slight wound. You will no doubt think it strange of me to write as I did write on Monday last, but I thought it wise not take part in a fierce hand to hand struggle. We had been informed four days previous to the event of what we had to do.

Our brigade was allotted to take three lines of trenches. It was October 12 when our Battalion paraded the streets in a typical French village. The day was a glorious one, the beautiful autumnal sun sending forth its rays whilst in the distance could be heard the booming of the big guns and over ahead the buzzing of aeroplanes."

Harrison describes the disappointment of being placed in the bombing party, as presumably he wanted fight alongside his own men. The text in the evening sentinel is rather illegible at this point so we will pick up where it becomes clear to read again.

"In the space of a few minutes a long line of dusty clad warriors were marching along that French road singing songs such as Bonnie Scotland and Tommy Atkins, others just whistling. Our tea consisted of bread and cheese and a little cake kindly supplied by JL. We talked about the coming events then after half an hour, the order came for us to fall in. I took the opportunity of wishing the boys the very best of luck and parted with a firm shake of their hands. As we recommenced our journey, we could hear the roar of the guns and see the rockets descending over the firing line. After about half an hour we arrived at a village devastated by fire. Here we had our orders and all the bombers set off with two bags of bombs per man. Another mile of tramping brought us to the communication trench. At this time we were in the firing line. When posted to my particular bay I sound slept till about 6am."[31]

---

[31] The Staffordshire evening sentinel, October 30th 1915 pp: 30.

On the 99th anniversary of the attack, October 13th 2014, the present day Sentinel published the account of Burslem's John Harrison in a tribute to him.

"At 8am on that notable morning, I enjoyed my last meal previous to the battle – a tin of meat and vegetables. You may guess I did justice to them. Moment and moment elapsed, our guns keeping a steady fire on the enemy position until noon, when they commenced a deafening thunder-like and hellish bombardment. The word was passed along to listen for orders.

Our Battalion was to go over first, and an order came. 'Have you got all the bombs'? 'Yes, all except otherwise detailed', came the reply.

I was one without, having been elected to carry a spade (my life saver). One O'clock arrived. Our guns still raining shells on the Germans. Another order: 'listen'. 'Gas helmets on'. These donned, our engineers commenced to give the Germans a taste of their own fat (gas). This practice continued until 1.45pm. A quarter of an hour – 10 minutes, then the Colonel arrived fully armed and wished us all good luck. Five minutes – two minutes – one minute.

A whistle 'blasts' and over the bridge of death we climbed and shouted. I got clear of our barbed wire and commenced to advance, rifle and bayonet fixed in one hand, and spade in the other, under a terrific machine gun fire, bullets whizzing past me in thousands. I got about 100 yards and took a short rest, up again, but alas, a bullet hit the spade, glanced off and grazed the bone above my left eye slightly. It dazed me for a minute, but I soon recovered myself, only to find that I was about 30 yards from the first German line (trench). Now I had to make the best of my way back.

I saw my left flank trench and made a dash for it, jumping clean into it, at which juncture I bandaged myself, still having the picture of the battlefield in my mind.

It was a desolate piece of ground, ploughed by artillery, swept by Maxim and rifle fire, covered with dead, wounded and dying. I caught sight of four Germans taking to their heels, fine, strapping fellows of the Prussian Guard, between their first and second lines. Before I was put out of action, I took aim, and one fell, then to my ill luck, if you can call it such, I fell before I had the pleasure of shooting another. After I had stopped the bleeding, I got the bandage on, and made my way down the whole firing line into the communication trench, and then direct to the first aid post. The sights I saw were simply heart-breaking. The shells were dropping all around us, throwing pieces of hot metal in all directions. The trenches were holding plenty of dead and wounded, some of the wounded were very bad, and in some cases I gave them water.

At last I arrived at the dressing station, enjoyed some cocoa and chocolate and had my wound attended to, after which I was taken to hospital in a bus, where I had some hot milk and bread and butter, and slept a deep sleep."[32]

Another in depth account of the charge came from a soldier from Woore, the following letter was written by Private W Weston, to his father.

"Just a line to let you know my wound is going well thanks to the doctors and sisters who have cared for me. We have had a very awful time from time we left the famous hill 60. We marched up and down the country then a course of bomb throwing had to be done by the whole Battalion. It was then the officers told us what was in front of us and every man took it as cheerfully as if he was going home on

---

[32] The Sentinel, Monday October 13th 2014 pp:17.

leave. Day after day passed and we were shown what had to be done. Then came the day for us to move from where we were billeted in a barn in a little village not far from the trenches. And wasn't it a march! At 12:20 midnight we landed after being pushed all over the place. Sleep, there was not any sleep for the trenches were packed out like rabbits. When day break broke we got our breakfast in the best way we would. All I had to eat was a tin of macaroni and that soon went. We idled the rest of the morning and on the stroke of mid-day our guns let the louts have some iron rations to share out the best way they could amongst them. The Germans did not forget us, though they sent us shell after shell, some doing damage, others not.

The game carried on for a good two hours then came our turn to do something. Every chap was merry Asif he had a £5 note promised him. At first gas and smoke bombs were thrown in scores. The gas and smoke began to get thicker and thicker and completely hid the German lines from view. I did not expect half the Huns would be left after the shelling we gave them, but before we had finished our two hours shelling the Germans had got, I should say about 20 machine guns in action and trained for the top of our parapet, and didn't they let us have it on the top thick and heavy. But what did we care? We knew what we were after, in spite of the dammed machine guns, and death was not to come to any man until he had done his duty, and then he gave up his life freely for the love of his country.

On the dot of five minutes past two the word came along, over the top lads, and the best of luck! Then the war cry went up… POTTERS FOR EVER! And no doubt you have seen it in the papers before. Over went our two lines of companies, and hell was let loose on the brave lads, for bullets were flying about like rain and down they went like corn in front of a scythe.

Then went over the top the remainder of the Battalion, except a party of bomb throwers. I was amongst these lads and we had to wait a while. Then our turn came and over we went with a bag of bombs, plus equipment, on we doubled. I went on and came to our barbed wire entanglements. I passed round the outside of the stakes and got in front of the wire and landed half way between our trenches and the Germans. Then wiz crack and I got hit. It was Asif a big hammer had hit when the bullet hit my left shoulder blade. The force of it swung me round like a top and I dropped like a log. I thought I was done. What brought me to my senses was a German coal box dropping about 30 yards from me. I bundled off m bombs and pack, left everything where I had dropped, even my rifle and bayonet and scrambled off to the right and ran in to an old communication trench running into our first line."

The Attack of 1/5th South Staffords

CAPT. W. MILLNER
(Killed)

Two companies of the 1/5th South Staffords, together with Numbers 3 and 4 Bombing Parties from the Battalion, were located in a communication trench to the east of Big Willie. The two companies had orders to wait for the first line of the 1/5th North Staffords to reach their position before advancing forward with them. The commander of "C" Company, Captain William Wistance, was able to observe that the 1/5th North Stafford's advance had been checked

---

[33] The Staffordshire advertiser, October 23rd 1915, pp:9

and his men remained in the trench. However, Captain William Millner, the officer commanding "B" Company, was unable to see the developing situation and therefore continued with his orders. The Company then climbed out from the trench and lay in front of it; No. 7 Platoon at the front, No.6 and No. 8 Platoons in the second line, waiting for the 1/5th North Staffords to arrive and link up with them. As they moved through the gaps cut in the barbed wire into the open, several men were hit by enfilade machine-gun fire from the Redoubt, and the German artillery began to shell the trench. Having suffered heavy casualties in this exposed position, the survivors were compelled to scramble back into the shelter offered by the trench. Among the casualties still lying out in the open was Captain Millner. 5351 Private Fred Proverbs climbed back over the parapet in an attempt to rescue his company commander. A shell killed both men while Proverbs was dressing Millner's wounds.

The man who tried to rescue Captain Millner was 5351 Private Fred Proverbs, of the 1/5th Battalion, The South Staffordshire Regiment. Known as Fritz to his friends, Fred Proverbs was a miner from Rawnsley and a Territorial for many years before the outbreak of the war, serving with "F" Company of the 5th Battalion, The South Staffordshire Regiment stationed at Hednesford. He was embodied at the outbreak of the war and arrived a Le Havre with "B" Company of the 1/5th South Staffords on 5 March 1915. On the 13 October 1915, he gave his life trying to save the life of his company commander, Captain William Millner, during the failed attack on the Hohenzollern Redoubt launched by "B" Company from "Big Willie" trench. The "Cannock Advertiser" reported that Private Proverbs had been killed, and the circumstances of his bravery, in two reports. On 23 October 1915, his death was recorded: "Private Fritz Proverbs (32) of the Hednesford Territorials, who lived with his widowed mother in Rawnsley, has been killed in action, the sad news being conveyed in a letter from his chum Private Will Gardner of Hazelslade. Private Proverbs has been three times previously wounded."

A week later, the paper interviewed one of his comrades who had returned to Cannock on leave:

SHOULD HAVE EARNED THE VICTORIA CROSS
How Private Fritz Proverbs Died Helping His Wounded Officer
"If ever a man should have earned the V.C. it was Private Fritz Proverbs", remarked Sergeant H. Willis of the Hednesford Territorials to an Advertiser representative on Tuesday morning. Proceeding, Sergeant Willis explained that after the successful attack on the Hohenzollern Redoubt, Pte. Proverbs got back to the trench quite safely. Captain Milner, who was lying wounded thirty yards from the trench called out that he wanted a field dressing. Without hesitation, Proverbs climbed over the parapet and dashed through a hail of bullets and flying shells to the wounded officer. He reached Captain Milner and was dressing the latters' wounds when he was struck and killed by shrapnel.
Fritz Proverbs has no known grave and is commemorated on the Loos Memorial. His name can also be found on the war memorial at Hednesford. Fritz's widowed mother was later awarded a grant by the Cannock and District Miner's Dependants Fund.

The second wave of the 1/5th South Staffords' attack, consisting of Battalion Headquarters, "A" Company and "D" Company, were positioned in the old British front line between Hulluch Alley and Border Alley. At 2.10 p.m., they attempted to cross over towards Big Willie to link up with the remainder of the Battalion.

9948 Corporal Howard Stott of "A" Company gave a vivid description of the assault:

"Promptly at two o'clock the order to advance came. Standing up in front of us our colonel, who appeared as calm as though he was merely taking part in manoeuvres at home – gave the word. As one man the company dashed forward. Never a lad held back, although all knew we were going to certain death. Then came the murderous hail of fire from the machine guns in the German trenches and the slaughter which took place in the next few minutes was terrible. We had to cross five or six hundred yards of open country, which was literally swept with machine-gun fire, before we reached our own front line parapet, and the poor fellows were simply mown down. Only two or three of us reached the German front trench."

9058 Private Benjamin Davis, a Wordsley soldier also serving with "A" Company, recalled his company's attempt to cross to "Big Willie":

"I was in the reserve trenches – some distance beyond the first line – with the result that we had to cover 300 yards in the open. You can imagine what it was like, with a murderous machine-gun fire against us. I had got about 200 yards when a bullet from a machine gun stuck me in the left hand. We were in the thick of it now, and I had to lie flat on the ground scarcely daring to breathe. There I stayed for an hour or so, until the fire had slackened, and then I started to crawl back to our lines, the bullets pinging around me…"

A soldier from Walsall, Sergeant Harry Smith, also took part in this advance with "C" Company:

"Over the parapets we went, but no sooner did we show ourselves than we were subjected to heavy machine-gun fire. Men dropped left and right, but the others never faltered. After receiving a slight wound in the arm, I fell to one in the back. Comrades who witnessed the attack said they had never seen lads go into it better."

Lieutenant Percy Slater watched the advance from the Battalion headquarters dugout of 1/6th South Staffords:

"It was wonderful seeing the great smoke-cloud along the front, and then five minutes before the bombardment stopped, the figures crawling over the parapet and lying down in front, as far as you could see either side. At the moment the guns lifted, all got up and began to run, or rather, jog. Then they all seemed to melt away."

None of the officers and only a handful of men from the two companies managed to reach their comrades in the forward trench, most of the survivors retiring back to the trenches from where the attack had begun. Of the two companies, only 18 men from "A" Company and 53 from "D" Company survived the advance unscathed. The men from these two companies that had managed to reach "Big Willie" Trench were reorganised under the command of Captain Wistance of "C" Company. Captain Leslie Cozens, the officer commanding "A" Company, was severely wounded during this attempt to advance and died the following day.

In a supporting role, the machine-gun teams waited for their turn to follow their comrades across the "Big Willie". However, as the advance faltered, their orders were changed. 9182 Private Benjamin Walford of the 1/5th South Staffords recalled the scene in the front line trench as his team moved to a new firing point:

"As we carried our gun along the trench we all had to stride across dead and wounded men. There was no time to think about these sad sights, our minds were concentrated on the one subject of getting a good position for the gun in order to keep the enemy back, for they were making an attempt to get across to our trench."

The photograph is of 9169 Corporal Jack Shipley of the 1/5th South Staffords, who came from Walsall and was an old boy of Queen Mary's Grammar School. Before going into action, he wrote to his parents:

"I am writing with very mixed feelings. I cannot say what may happen but whatever comes I shall not budge. If I do not return from the attack think of me as doing my duty - not a slacker."

Jack was killed in the attack, aged 21. He has no known grave and is commemorated on the Loos Memorial.

The Support Battalions Attempt to Advance – 1/6th South Staffords and 1/6th North Staffords on 13 October 1915

It was now the turn of the third assault wave to try to reach the first objective. The companies moved forward from their assembly point in the support trenches to the front line, which was choked with the wounded and dead of the previous two attacks. "A" Company, (Captain John Thursfield) and "C" Company, (Captain William Parkes) led 1/6th South Staffords attack following in the wake of the 1/5th South Staffords. 2884 Private Ronald Lerry, with the rest of "A" Company, prepared to climb the parapet:

"With eager eyes we watched a line of men move forward on the left, then more lines of men come on, and the time for us to start quickly came. Another Battalion was leading, and we immediately followed from the support trench. We had a considerable distance to go, and the country was very open. As soon as we got up we found ourselves under a heavy fire of shrapnel, machine gun, and rifle bullets. The ground all round was being ploughed up. Soon comrades began to fall. Whilst we went along we saw some here and there who had already been knocked out, dead and dying. That was the sickening part of it. Although one only had a hurried glance at such sights during that battle-rush, they impressed themselves on one more than all the murderous fire we were facing. At the time one hardly noticed that, and we were all quite cool in the face of it. I noticed our officer, Mr. Yeatman, very coolly light a cigarette as we lay down during the advance. It did not take long to reach our own front trench, which we cleared at a jump and went forward at a steady double."

2466 Lance-Corporal Walter Shotton, another soldier from Wolverhampton, also took part in "A" Company's advance:

"As soon as the Battalion started to get out of the trenches the machine guns played on them. We in the rear scrambled out of our trenches, and five yards away lay down until we were all ready. We had our coats rolled on our backs, but most of us threw them away, so that we could run faster. We made our first rush of twenty yards or more, and as we did so the machine gun bullets struck many of us. Then we had another rush to the second line of trenches. The machine guns were effective again. Lieutenant Finnis, who was leading, was shot through the leg, but he shouted "Never mind me, Go on, boys! Go on!" And we went. A shell burst in front of me, a piece of shrapnel struck my nose, another piece knocked my rifle out of my hand, the concussion of the air blew me six feet high, and when I dropped I twisted my knee. But I stumbled along and, as I jumped down into the trench a bullet went through my hat."

About seventy men from the two forward companies of the 1/6th South Staffords had managed to reach as far as Point 57 of Hulluch Alley, where they linked up with the remnants of the 1/5th South Staffords. Walter Shotton was among the survivors:

"When we got to our first line of trenches we were considerably reduced in numbers, both in officers and men, and we found that the South had not been able to advance owing to the machine gun fire along their parapet as soon as they tried to get out. When we reached them we all had another go, but the one or two who managed it were killed before they got very far."

The forward companies of the 1/6th North Staffords, "A" and "B" Companies, also came up against withering machine gun fire as they attempted to advance across the open ground in the wake of the 1/5th North Staffords. Company-Quartermaster-Sergeant E. Martin of "B"

Company gave a stirring account of his unit's exploits to his local newspaper in Uttoxeter:

Exactly at the appointed time the signal to advance was given, and Major Peach, who was in command of the company, was first out of the trench. Then the advance began across the open, the men moving as if on parade. The forward movement was well maintained, although men were falling fast for the first 300 yards, when Captain Bamford fell. He was last heard shouting "Come on, lads!" The first position was reached and it was won by the bulldog courage of the men, and was held with more than bulldog tenacity.

The reality of the situation was that while a few men from the forward companies had managed to reach the communications trench connected to Big Willie, most of the survivors were compelled to return to the trenches from where the attack had started. Major Edwin Peach, the Officer Commanding "B" Company of the 1/6th North Staffords, was wounded during the advance. In a letter written from a hospital in London, he recounted how he was rescued and taken to safety:

"I was hit early in the attack while leading my men, of whom I am very proud. They were as cool as if on parade, and charged at quick time. I had a fearfully painful time getting back about 300 yards in the open, crawling with my leg dragging behind, expecting to be hit again every minute. My servant Wilkinson stayed with me like a brick, and lifted up the barbed wire entanglements so that I could get under. Then he bound the leg with two pieces of board to stop it wobbling and carried me on his back for two miles to the Dressing Station, where Colonel Dent set my leg."

Private A. J. Edwards had seen the fate of the first two waves and prepared to face the onslaught of machine-gun fire and artillery:

"The poor chaps of the 5th were simply mown down. Then we followed and were served just the same. It was sickening, but, of course, there was no such thing as turning back, so on went, capturing a trench the Germans called "Big Willie", and a noted redoubt. There were not many of us left by the time we got there, but we stuck to them like glue, until we were reinforced. The Germans, although their machine guns were playing havoc with us, started running away like mad. A great many of them have finished running now, because they are 'land-owners'."

The fourth wave of 137th Brigade's assault consisted of "B" Company (Captain Ernest Cresswell – wounded and missing) and "D" Company (Captain W. A. Adam - wounded), of 1/6th South Staffords, and 'C' and 'D' Companies of the 1/6th North Staffords. They were ordered to move from their assembly trench to the front line as planned. However, due to the chaotic conditions in the communication trenches, they were compelled to advance across the open to reach the forward trenches. Sergeant George Norton later described the events that followed in a letter to his brother Sydney:

CAPT. JENKINSON
(Killed)

"As soon as my platoon got over, I had Cpl Fradley shot dead. The next I saw was Private Marsh badly bleeding. He asked me not to leave him. I called for stretcher bearers. Next I saw Captain Jenkinson shot through the leg. He fell and the stretcher bearers came to him, and they were also shot down. One was killed - Pte. Neville of my platoon - three were wounded. The next I saw was Staff Sergt. Platts and Kenney shot and several more."

---

[34] The Staffordshire advertiser, October 30th 1915, pp:9

Lance-Corporal Maurice Ewers, from Horninglow, also advanced with "C" Company. His brother Leonard was also a Lance-Corporal in the same company:

"As we had a long way to go before reaching our objective, we just went at the quick – not the double – going forward a short distance and the falling prone, and then forward again. We lost our Captain – one of the best officers we could wish for – quite early. We were all lying down when Captain Jenkinson got up to give an order. It was a brave thing to do, but he was hit and fell, and I believe he was hit a second time."

Lance-Corporal Francis Clement, from Tamworth, also took part in "C" Company's forward movement:

"With a yell, "C" Company went over the top with brave Capt. Jenkinson in front. As we were going over the top two of my section were killed and about a dozen altogether fell before we had gone many yards, but still we kept going while the bullets flew about like hailstones. My rifle was smashed by a bullet but I managed to pick up a dead man's gun. We couldn't avoid walking over the dead, who lay about like sheep."

The two companies suffered heavy casualties in their rush across to the front-line trench, particularly amongst officers, as Lance-Corporal Maurice Ewers recounted:

"After Captain Jenkinson was put out of action, Lieut. J.M. Stack, the next in command, was hit in both legs. Then Lieut. Paget took charge. He was just saying, "If you can advance another 50 yards…" when he was shot in the groin. He was succeeded by Second-Lieutenant Collis, who got through alright, eventually reaching the trench uninjured. As a matter of fact this young officer had been hit on the fingers by shrapnel quite early on, but he pluckily went through the action, ignoring the injury."

With the officers becoming casualties, the task of maintaining the momentum of the attack devolved to the Non-Commissioned Officers, amongst them Sergeant George Norton:

"I then advanced into the first line trench. I found about all the officers had been shot. I got my men together then rushed into the second line trench without losing a man in my platoon on the second rush. I think there was a great mistake in rushing the first time in short rushes. We lost a lot of men by doing so. A rush straight across would have been a success. We were all exposed to fire. I dropped into a shell hole. I stopped in the first trench for about ten minutes. I told the men to prepare to advance into the next line of trenches about two hundred yards away without halting and they did. I was very pleased to know all got across without a man getting hit."

However, Maurice Ewers saw his brother Leonard fall during this rush:

"My own brother was killed before my eyes. He had gone 200 yards and was getting near the fire trench parapet when a bullet put an end to his life. He fell back into the trench, and was wedged in the bottom. Mercifully, it was almost instantaneous death. I do not know if he instinctively realised that anything was going to happen to him, but he had left his belongings in his valise, and had made out a sort of supplementary will."

On arriving at the front line, the remaining troops of the companies forming the fourth wave were ordered to remain in position to defend it against German counter-attacks. Sergeant George Norton found that the front line was in a state of utter confusion as dead and wounded mingled together, making any further attempts to advance impossible:

"I then got an order from Colonel Radcliff to hold this trench. So this stopped us from advancing any further. Here I found us all mixed up with all sorts of Regiments, South and North Staffords, Lincolns and Leicesters. We were having it very hot with bombs but we gave them more than they gave us. It was a fine bit of work to see young Schofield of my platoon running the Germans up the communications trench with bombs. I never expected him to come back but he did in an awful sweat - he had used all his bombs."

In the space of about ten minutes, the Brigade had been decimated and the remnants of the Staffordshire Battalions had not made any progress against the defenders of the Hohenzollern Redoubt. The 138th Brigade's attack had met with some success, although the Lincolns and Leicesters had also suffered heavy losses. Despite this, a foothold had been gained in the Redoubt but due to the failure of the Stafford's assault, their position was vulnerable and heavy fighting was to continue there for the next two days. Old sections of German trench were opened and eventually linked with the sap dug by sappers of 1/1st North Midland Field Company and the pioneers of 1/1st Monmouths. A telephone cable was then laid along the trench, allowing communications to be established with the troops located in the Redoubt.

BOMBERS BATTLE

The Bombers' Battle – The Fight for Big Willie Trench

The Bombers in action.

Whilst the infantry of the assault waves made their attempts to advance across to their first objectives, the bombing parties of 137th Brigade were engaged in a ferocious battle to link up with 138th Brigade in the Hohenzollern Redoubt. At 2 o'clock, Number 5 Bombing Party of 1/6th North Staffords, led by Second-Lieutenant Harold Beaufort, the Brigade Bombing Officer, commenced their attack up Big Willie Trench and had managed to advance approximately thirty yards up the trench towards the redoubt. The party got as far as a second trench block but as the casualties started to mount up, and under a fierce German counter-attack, the survivors were forced to withdraw back to the barricade from where they started. At this critical time, the position of the Brigade's dump of grenades became a cause of concern to Beaufort. He had given instructions for supplies of grenades to be brought up to Big Willie in order to maintain a ready supply for use in continuing the bombing attack to their next objective. As a result of the failure to take Big Willie Trench, Beaufort feared that the supply could now be destroyed during a counter-attack by German bombers. As he was moving back down the communication trench to issue new orders to his bombers, Second-Lieutenant Beaufort was killed.

A second attempt was then made to advance up Big Willie Trench by Number 4 Bombing Party from 1/5th South Staffords, commanded by Lieutenant Hubert Hawkes. The bombers succeeded in pushing back the German defenders using both grenades and their bayonets. Eventually, the second trench block was reached and the 1/5th South Staffords began to consolidate their position, frantically pulling down the battered parapet of the trench to improve the barricade. A bombing party from the 1/6th South Staffords also arrived in Big Willie Trench and was actively engaged in defending the position until virtually the entire contingent became casualties. Some bombers may have advanced further, but this could not be confirmed, as Major Law reported:

"I observed signalling from the "Dump" for more bombs and S.A.A.; also later for reinforcements. At the time I took the signal to be from our advanced bombing line but I could not convince myself that they should have arrived there."

Private Harold Holden, of "A" Company of the 1/6th North Staffords, was a member of Number 6 Bombing Party:

"At five minutes past two we all mounted the parapet, most of us feeling mad – some wild with thirst for German blood. Then I witnessed the most awful sight I ever saw in all my life. Hundreds fell before we reached the German lines and then didn't we let into them. I cannot describe what I saw, as I was too excited. Later we got reinforced, as almost all of our officers had either been killed or wounded. I got back into our own trench, thanking God…"

Number 6 Bombing Party also suffered heavy casualties during their attack, with the detachment commander, Second-Lieutenant Norman Joseph, being wounded. Private Holden was also injured during the action:

"The trench was full of fellows, either dead or wounded, and amidst all this I heard the cry for 'stretcher-bearers', and of course I wandered off to where the cry came from. Eventually I found it was a poor chap who was hit with a shell, and he was lying helpless in front of our trench exposed to the Germans, who were firing like mad. I had been spared up to then, and then without hesitating I jumped over the parapet, and before I could say a word I was shot in the thick part of my right leg. I was compelled to fall back into our trench, as the pain was awful."

The two bombing parties of 1/6th South Staffords were also heavily engaged in conducting bombing attacks. Unable to attack towards Slag Alley and Dump Trench as originally planned, the bombers joined in with supporting the attack up Big Willie Trench. Lieutenant Gerald Howard Smith, together with Sergeants William Bratt and Fred Watson, led their parties into the trench and soon became engaged in the fierce fighting.

At about 2.30 p.m., the Germans mounted a counter-attack against the trench block in Big Willie Trench. Sergeant Joseph Beards and a section from 'C' Company of the 1/5th South Staffords defended the barrier. Beards and his section became involved in a brutal struggle to hold their position, both sides using their bayonets and throwing grenades. Lieutenant Hawkes, alerted to the dangerous situation at the barrier, brought forward Number 4 Bombing Party to reinforce the defenders. A group of German infantry was seen trying to advance over the open ground in an attempt to cut off Sergeant Beard's group. "C" Company's No. 10 Platoon quickly lined the parapet of the trench and engaged the advancing Germans with rapid rifle fire. A Sergeant from Walsall witnessed the action:

"A few of the enemy found their way down an old communications trench, and got within ten yards of our barbed wire, from where they threw bombs. From our 'bay' we potted at them and bombed them out. Our trench was attacked on the left by the Germans, who were trying to force a barricade. We continued bomb-throwing until darkness came on. There was heavy and continuous artillery fire all the time."

Faced with this determined defence, and having taken several casualties, the Germans were forced to withdraw. After a brief lull, another attack was then made on the barricade in Big Willie Trench. Sergeant Beards, assisted by Private W. Barnes, was again compelled to defend the position at bayonet point. Beards received a wound to the head during this encounter but refused to leave the barricade. The Germans were now advancing in strength down the remains of the trench and continued to shower Beards and Barnes with grenades. At about 4.00 p.m., the two men were forced to make a fighting withdrawal after Germans began to attack from three directions with grenades. No support was available due to heavy casualties among the bombing parties, but they continued to fight tenaciously. Sergeant Fred Watson of the 1/6th South Staffords continued to hold his position against German attacks for five hours until he was killed. Lieutenant Hawkes was later awarded the Military Cross and Sergeant Beards the Distinguished Conduct Medal for the actions in Big Willie Trench.

While the actions in Big Willie Trench were taking place, carrying parties tried to bring up more supplies of small arms ammunition and grenades, but were hampered by the narrow communication trenches being clogged with casualties, as witnessed by Private Benjamin Walford and his machine-gun team:

"There was a constant cry for bombs – thousands must have been used on one point alone."

There was a shortage of Mills Bombs available at the supply dumps and a wide variety of types, including rifle grenades and bombs without detonators or fuses, were sent up to the units of 46th Division. Most of these proved to be useless.

Maintaining communications with Brigade and Divisional Headquarters during the assault was a trying task for the Battalion signallers. Their job was made extremely difficult due to the chaotic conditions in the assault trenches and broken wires caused by German artillery fire, as Lance-Corporal George Dunn of the 1/5th South Staffords recounted:

"I had one of my worst experiences during the reciprocal bombardment. I had to go out to repair the lines; the communications had broken, and I had to find the break. Just at that point I saw two of our men had been killed by a shell, and at once the fear came that one might be my brother Arthur, who is also in the Brierley Hill Company. I repaired the broken line and then found that the two unfortunate men were evidently machine-gunners."

Private Thomas Pursell, a Wolverhampton man serving with the Signal Section of 1/6th South Staffords, wrote:

"I was very fortunate, as I was one of the reserve telephone section to go over the parapet, as the first section could not get into communication. We were rushing up the communication trench to the first trench to see if we were needed when we met our signal officer, who had just been wounded through the wrist. He ordered us back to the second line to await orders. Fortunately, communications kept good and we were not needed to go over to the advanced point."

END OF THE DAY

137th Brigade's Attack Fails

By 4 o'clock, the fighting on the 137th Brigade front had virtually ceased, with both sides conducting an artillery duel over the area, while the Lincolns, Leicester's and Monmouth's were engaged in a bitter struggle to hold onto their foothold in the Hohenzollern Redoubt against determined German counter-attacks. A thick mist had begun to descend over the battlefield as dusk settled. The priority of those troops who remained uninjured was to prepare their positions for defence against German counter-attacks. Efforts were made to reorganise the remaining Staffords by the surviving officers. Major Law reported that:

"All the men that that could be collected were pushed up to the fire trenches, which at times were very thin in places.

About a dozen men were kept back for passing bombs up the communication trenches, which had become badly blocked with wounded."

The survivors of the 1/5th South Staffords positioned in Big Willie Trench received further reinforcements when a detachment of bombers from 1/6th Sherwood Foresters, led by Captain Victor Robinson, reached their position. The defences were then reorganised. The Sherwood Foresters positioned themselves on the right flank. Holding the centre sections of the line were the combined "B" and "D" Companies of the 1/5th South Staffords, under the command of Captain Edgar Wilson and a detachment of twenty-two men from 1/6th South Staffords, led by Captain John Thursfield. The left flank, closest to the Hohenzollern Redoubt, was entrusted to the survivors of "A" and "C" Companies of the 1/5th South Staffords, led by Captain William Wistance.

Considerable numbers of casualties, both dead and wounded, choked the assembly trenches in the Brigade's frontage but little could be done to help. The walking wounded were able to make their own way to the first aid post in Bart's Alley, but those who were more seriously injured had to wait in agony until they could be taken to the Collecting Station, as Sergeant George Norton observed:

"I walked along the trench. I witnessed a terrible sight of men killed and wounded and no stretcher bearers to be found. Men were in awful pain. I dressed a lot of wounds and then sent them out of the trench. Them that could not walk had to lie in the trench in awful pain for twelve to eighteen hours or more."

His brother, Sergeant Sydney Norton, had been wounded during the attack but managed to crawl back to the trenches. He later recalled his experience in a letter to his wife in Fazeley:

"I crept about 200 yards on my stomach into a safe place where the stretcher bearers could get me expecting every minute was my last. As I was being carried away they were pinging away at us but oh when I was in a safe place I prayed and thanked the Lord above. I could see him on my right and you and the children on my left."

The ground in front of the first line trenches was littered with dead, dying and wounded soldiers. Some of the wounded had managed to find temporary sanctuary in the comparative safety of shell-holes but others, like Private Joseph Barlow were dangerously exposed:

"There I lay flat, face downwards, wondering what would happen next. A few yards away lay seven or eight pals, some dead, some gone delirious. I felt sorrier for them than I did myself. I could not help crying and praying for the Lord to help them. You should have seen me digging a hole with my chin in the soft ground. I couldn't get low enough, the bullets were flying within an inch at times."

LIEUT. MAYER
(Killed).

Second-Lieutenant Frank Mayer had been wounded in the leg whilst leading No. 4 Platoon of "B" Company of the 1/5th North Staffords in the first wave of the attack. Hearing the cries of a wounded soldier for water, Mayer had crawled over to him to give him a drink. Moments later, Frank Mayer was shot in the head and killed. His body was seen still clasping his water bottle. The plight of the wounded was too much to bear for some soldiers. Seeing their friends lying helpless out in the open compelled many men to try and bring them back into the trenches, despite being ordered not to do so. For some this proved to be a fatal decision. Private Walter Shotton saw two of his comrades from the 1/6th South Staffords, Privates Archie Marr and Rowland Tonks, killed during attempts to reach wounded soldiers. Drummer John Clarke, an eighteen-year old soldier from Burton, made three attempts to rescue wounded soldiers. The first man he brought back died on reaching the trench, but he was able to recover two wounded soldiers successfully. Clarke was fatally wounded when making a fourth attempt and died a few hours later. Sergeant George Norton witnessed another Burtonian, Lance-Corporal Fred Mallett, and attempted to bring in wounded comrades:

"He had been over the top and fetched in two wounded. I begged him not to go over again. He would not be persuaded by me. He went - did not go far before he was hit never to rise again. It was a case of several men throwing their lives away trying to save the wounded, but it was murder to go."

As night fell, Private Joseph Barlow had been lying wounded in the open for about four hours when he decided to try and reach the British trenches:

"After dark I thought I would risk my neck and try and get back to our trenches. I unbuckled my belt and gradually took all my equipment off (about ½ cwt.), and crawled on my stomach, keeping low and acting dead when their flare lights were up. Got to our barbed wire, crawling under it got my tunic fast; loosened it, got up and ran the other ten yards like a March hare, and plunged head first into the trench, wounds or no wounds. Then I started off as well as I could hobble, stumbling and striding over dead and dying."

Sadly, for some of the wounded help came too late. Second-Lieutenant Tom Dann of the 1/6th South Staffords had received a severe wound from a bullet that entered his thigh and exited through his foot. Men from his Battalion brought in Dann during the night but no help could be given to him and he slowly bled to death in the trench. Sergeant George Norton was involved in the recovery of his company commander, Captain John Jenkinson:

By this time it was getting dark, and I thought it was a good opportunity to get in some of the wounded we could. First we got in Capt. Jenkinson (Talbot helped). He lay in the open for several hours for it would have been certain death to have gone out to him. After a struggle we got him in. It was a case of being cruel to be kind. As he lay on the fire step, he asked for a doctor. We could not do anything, for there was not an ambulance man to be found. We made him as comfortable as we could. I could see he had been hit again, for he had an awful wound in his stomach. I watched over him. I could see he could not last long. He lasted about an hour. Then we put him in a small disused trench close by. We covered him over.

The 137th (Staffordshire) Brigade are Withdrawn - 13-15 October 1915

German trench mortars and artillery shells continued to bombard the British trenches during the night as the shattered survivors of 137th Brigade held their positions. Expectant of an imminent German counter-stroke, half of the troops stood-to in preparation to repulse any attack while their comrades tried to snatch some rest. Private Benjamin Walford was with his machine-gun during the night when he received some much-needed sustenance:

"During the night it became calmer, and what a relief it was! We were getting spent. About 1.00 a.m. an officer brought round some rum for us. He gave us a drink out of one of those small collapsible cups. It absolutely burnt our throats, but it was acceptable, for we were parched and could hardly speak for want of a drink. Do you know, we had one bottle of water to last us three days; and all the food we had was in our haversacks, which we had taken with us from the barn."

Sergeant George Norton recalled that:

"It was an awful night, foggy and damp. The enemy tried a counter-attack but were repulsed. At daybreak they continued to shell us. I found out that Sergt. Hayward had been hit by a shell but did not see him. All day long we stuck to the trench expecting a counter-attack, but it was an artillery duel all day long. About four o'clock we had news that we were going to be relieved at nine o'clock, but unfortunately did not get relieved until seven the next morning by the Guards."

On the morning of 14 October, Brigadier Feetham went up to inspect the trenches that were held by his Brigade. He informed the remaining officers that the Guards Division would relieve them that night. In Big Willie Trench, a company from 1/5th Sherwood Foresters arrived at 6.15 a.m. to take over from "A" and "C" Companies of the 1/5th South Staffords on the left flank. The Foresters were to support a renewed attempt to attack up the German-held section of Big Willie to link up with an assault made from the West Face of the Hohenzollern Redoubt. The attack took place but was beaten back by the determined German defenders. At mid-day, the detachment from 1/6th South Staffords withdrew from Big Willie to join the remainder of the Battalion in the front-line trenches before they were relieved. Private Benjamin Walford's machine-gun team were also relieved and began to make their way back down the communication trenches towards Vermelles:

"We were relieved by other details during the afternoon of the day after the attack. We had to take all our guns with us. It was a long journey to get out and they didn't forget to shell us even then. They were bent on giving us a good send-off."

The conditions in the shattered trenches made the relief of 137th Brigade by 3rd Guards Brigade extremely difficult. The Guards found the positions they had left three days before much changed from when 46th Division had relieved them in preparation for their attack. The positions were now littered with the detritus of war; empty gas cylinders, smashed rifles, discarded equipment and the bodies of the dead, some partially buried by artillery fire. Such was the congestion in the line that the Staffords had to wait until the morning of 15th October until the troops from the 3rd Guards Brigade fully took over from them. As the Guards filed into the trenches, Sergeant George Norton recalled the scene as the shattered remains of 137th Brigade withdrew.

"I shall never forget that Saturday morning when we left the trenches. The spectacle presented was that of a true battlefield. In a tangle of torn barbed wire were to be seen the scattered bodies of the slain - many of them being held up more or less in an upright position. Next we had the order to file out. I had to get to the rear and see every man what was left was out of the trench. The Guards took over duties."

"I believe our Division got cut up very badly"

The Immediate Aftermath of the 46th Division's Attack on the Hohenzollern Redoubt

The attack on the Hohenzollern Redoubt had been a shattering experience for the Territorials from Staffordshire. None of 137th Brigade's objectives had been captured, the assault having been halted almost as soon as it had begun by a combination of concentrated artillery and machine gun fire.

The 138th (Lincoln and Leicester) Brigade had managed to take and secure part of the Redoubt but this limited success had been achieved at high cost. 139th (Sherwood Foresters) Brigade had also fought desperately to hold onto the small gains made in the Redoubt. In the days following the attack, the commanding officers of the Battalions and the Brigade Commanders wrote reports for Major General Montague-Stuart-Wortley, who in turn composed his own account based on his observations and those of his subordinates.

Several factors were attributed as having contributed to the failure of 137th Brigade's attack. The artillery bombardment had been too light and failed to suppress German resistance in the sector, particularly the machine gun emplacements located in the Redoubt and the ruins of Fosse 8. Although the main barrage had begun at mid-day, the heavy artillery deployed for the operation had been ordered to bombard the Corons de Pekin, Corons de Maroc, Pentagon Redoubt and the Dump for only ten minutes from 1.00 p.m. For the remaining 50 minutes prior to the attack, the heavy guns shelled communications trenches and provided counter-battery fire. Both Lieutenant Colonel Raymer of the 1/5th South Staffords and Lieutenant Colonel Law of the 1/6th South Staffords reported that machine gun fire was directed at their assembly trenches in the minutes prior to the assault, and that the fire came mainly from the Dump and the South Face of the Redoubt. In his report, Major General Montague-Stuart-Wortley wrote:

"There appears no doubt that the bombardment directed on BIG WILLIE, SOUTH FACE and DUMP trench, that is the trenches immediately in front of the right attack was not effective.

There was continual sniping of our trenches during the whole of the bombardment, and from 1.15 p.m. onwards, there were continual bursts of machine gun and rifle fire from the above- mentioned trenches and from the DUMP. On the conclusion of the bombardment the enemy so far from being shaken, got up and fired over their parapets freely, their trenches appeared strongly held."

The supply of grenades was also considered to be a significant factor in the failure to hold sections of the German line captured earlier during the attack, an assertion supported by the Official History:

"…what the British won was lost again for lack of a sufficient supply of effective hand-grenades."

The grenade was considered the best weapon to use for close-quarter fighting, particularly when attacking along trenches and in defending positions against counter-attacks. Although it had been specified that only Mills Bombs would be used by the Division's bombing parties, the supplies available were insufficient and other types were sent up to the forward troops, often without detonators. This certainly affected the 138th Brigade, which were compelled to withdraw from sections of the Redoubt that they had captured when German bombing attacks overwhelmed their defences. J. D. Hills, the author of the 1/5th Leicester's Battalion History, considered that the officer responsible for this mistake should have been shot. In the case of 137th Brigade, the bombing parties experienced shortages of grenades, but the major factors in their failure to secure the objectives were the heavy casualties suffered by the bombers and the lack of reinforcements available to consolidate the gains made in Big Willie.

The 46th Division had 180 Officers and 3,583 Other Ranks killed, wounded and missing between 13 and 15 October, with 137th Brigade's casualties totalling 68 Officers and 1,478 Other Ranks. The breakdown of casualties between the four infantry Battalions was:

1/5th South Staffordshire:
13 Officers and 306 Other Ranks

1/6th South Staffordshire:
18 Officers and 389 Other Ranks

1/5th North Staffordshire:
20 Officers and 485 Other Ranks

1/6th North Staffordshire:
17 Officers and 298 Other Ranks

The casualties suffered by Staffordshire's Territorial Force units during their attack on the Hohenzollern Redoubt had ravaged the ranks. All of the infantry Battalions suffered heavy casualties, with the 1/5th Battalion, The North Staffordshire Regiment having the highest number of all of the units of 46th Division. Of over 700 officers and men that entered the line on the night of 12 October, scarcely two hundred returned from the trenches when the Battalion was relieved. Sergeant G.C. Norton described the situation in the 1/6th Battalion, The North Staffordshire Regiment in a letter to his brother, Sydney Norton:

"Our Battalion lost heavily. I was the only Sergt that came out without a scratch. In fact all the Officers and N.C.O.'s suffered a lot. There were only three officers, with the Colonel and the Adjutant, came out of it. Sergt. Copeland,

Sergt. Hair, Sergt. Cutler, Sergt. Stone were killed and others wounded - yourself, Platts, Austin, Kenney, Hammond, Watts, Shirley, Cpl. Burrows, Clements, Littleford, Cronise - I cannot remember them all. Samuel Smith has died of his wound, also Mason. You will be surprised to see the list of the lot. We had a roll call the next morning. I shall never forget it - the strengths were 'A' Company - 90, 'B' - 92, 'C' - 112, 'D' - 114."

The reconstruction process was swift enough to allow the Staffordshire units of 46th Division to re-enter the line by the beginning of November 1915 without having to resort to temporary amalgamations, as had occurred with several Territorial Force Battalions following the Second Battle of Ypres. On receiving the news of the losses, a draft of 130 soldiers was directly sent from the Territorial Base Depot at Rouen to replace the losses sustained by the 1/5th Battalion, The North Staffordshire Regiment. Their 3/5th Battalion based at Belton Park also immediately despatched a draft of 18 Officers and 250 Other Ranks to Rouen as replacements. Although drafts soon brought units back up to strength, it can be detected in that many survivors felt that the losses sustained had changed their unit irrevocably. The authors of one unit history made the telling observation that the casualties suffered by the Territorials had been devastating and

"A valuable fighting force received a blow from which it was destined to recover but slowly".

On 16th October 1915, Major-General E. J. Montague-Stuart-Wortley, General Officer Commanding 46th (North Midland) Division, wrote to all of the County Territorial Force Associations that administered the units under his command:

"I should be obliged if you would inform the President and members of your Association that in a recent attack on the enemy's position the North Midland Division behaved with distinguished gallantry, worthy of the best traditions of the British Army.

"I trust that their example may arouse enthusiasm in their various counties and as a result of their gallant efforts may bring every able-bodied man into the ranks.

I am proud to command a division composed of officers and other ranks who, for love of King and country, have sacrificed private interests, and whose example should be widely followed by every man imbued with patriotic sentiments."

Lord Dartmouth, the Lord-Lieutenant of Staffordshire, responded:

"As chairman for the County Territorial Force Association, and speaking on their behalf, as one who, through ill report and good report, has never doubted the possibilities of the Territorial Force when their opportunity came, let me say that we are proud today to find that the Force we helped to raise has more than justified our most sanguine expectations"

With the praise of the men from those in high places or higher ranks, it could become easy to think that was the end of their ordeal, but for the survivors, there was one more peril. They had to try and recover the dead and find the missing. During the Gallipoli campaign there was an informal truce, so both sides could venture out into no man's land to try and recover bury their dead. The reason being, the hot Turkish sun had created a stench so unbearable something had to be done. There was no informal truce at Loos, but as this article from the Sentinel shows, the British troops did try and recover their dead, only this too was to become a very dangerous task.

THE DEAD STILL ON THE BATTLE FIELD

BURIAL PARTIES FIRED AT.

Mr C Valentine Williams, special correspondent of the "Daily Mail" writing from the General headquarters of the British Army on Sunday describing the order which is being brought into the Hohenzollern Redoubt by its British occupants and went on to say...

Think of anything you will that will suggest squalor and desolation- the refuse heaps of an industrial town, a London canal bank, a mouldering and neglected cemetery, you will not hit upon anything that approaches the utter chaos and abandonment of which our men are evolving some kind of order in the Hohenzollern Redoubt.

They have rebuilt the parapet of the trenches to face the other way, against the enemy, with German sandbags as gautly as Joseph's coat, brown and blue and green and red or stripy, mostly made from the cheapest shoddy, nothing like the soil and business like sacking of the British sandbags. Behind the traverse protecting the work from the rear fire which when the Germans were here was the parapet facing the first German line with the British lines beyond that. The chaos is indescribable. I can enumerate some of the objects lying among the shell holes, the broken barbed wire, the splintered Chevaux de frise, the rusting rifles and bayonets, many of the latter stained crimson with coagulated blood. Parts of uniforms, caps, mess tins, unexploded bombs, cartridges by the thousand, letters, knives, but I cannot convey the squalor of it all.

The dead lie amid the chaos. These are our sacred dead, the men who gave their lives for the trench in which I stand. The German dead you cannot see with a periscope for they are lying beyond the parapet in the space between the British and enemy lines. Our men lie ridged in their khaki as they fell, as though some are sleeping on the grass, their rifles often clasped in their out reached hands.

In places they lie singly, elsewhere in groups. In many cases a friendly hand had cast a grey coat or waterproof sheet over their faces. Out men in the front line bury them as they can, and roughly made crosses here and there with inscriptions in illegible pen mark their graves. But the Germans fire indiscriminately on all burial parties so that this pious work can only be performed dully.[35]

For those reading back home this would have made very grim reading, not only desolation described but also the growing possibility that their loved ones, if found , may never receive a proper burial, due to being interrupted by the Germans firing at them.

Coverage of the attack in the Evening sentinel began on October 16th 1915, reporting the words of Field-Marshall Sir John French, Which had had released to the press on October 14th.

---

[35] The Staffordshire weekly Sentinel, October 30th 1915.

LATEST WAR NEWS.

SIR J. FRENCH'S REPORT.

The British Advance.

The following telegraphic despatch, dated General Headquarters, 7 52 pm., Thursday, October 14th, has been received from Field-Marshal Sir John French :

"Yesterday (Wednesday) afternoon, after bombardment, we attacked the enemy's trenches under cover of a cloud of smoke and gas from a point about 600 yards south west of Hulluch to the Hohenzollern Redoubt.

We gained about a thousand yards of trench just south and west of Hulluch, but were unable to maintain our position there owing to enemy shell fire. We captured the main trench of the Hohenzollern Redoubt but the enemy are still in communication trenches between the Redoubt and the quarries."[36]

In these early days of the news reaching the families back home, there is no mention of any individuals killed, given the chaos and confusion of the attack it is easy to suggest that they simply had no idea who had lived and who had died, until an official role call was carried out. Another factor would be not to tell the truth as this would break the moral of both the troops and their families back home. At the beginning of the Battle of Loos the Author Rudyard

---

[36] The Staffordshire evening Sentinel, October 16th 1915 pp:7

Kipling, one of the Great Wars propagandists argued against the act of hiding the true cost of war as he believed that if the British public knew how many had fallen as soon as possible, they would be angered and men would join up for revenge, or at least the women would encourage any healthy men still living in Britain to go and avenge their fallen towns folk.

Those in power knew of the great losses that took place during the Battle of Loos, and this becomes all too apparent when the evening sentinel published an URGENT NEED FOR RECRUITS. The Mayor of Newcastle under Lyme was accompanied by a Mr Dr Shuffelbottom, who gave a stirring speech in mid-October 1915.

Dr Shuffelbottom said

"It seemed strange that after 14 months of war at a time of Great national crisis, they should still have to appeal for more men. They all should know of the great advance which had been made recently along the western front, that the Germans had been pushed back trench after trench and in some cases mile after mile. But at what cost. There was scarcely a town of village in the country and in some cases scarcely a home which had not suffered loss. The letters he had received showed that the fighting around Loos and Hill 70 had been as terrific as anything in military history and it was because of the sacrifice the Gallant lads had made that men were being asked to come forward and support their brothers in the fighting line. It was not a question of should they go or not, it was a question of when should they go."[37]

---

[37] The Staffordshire evening sentinel October 16th 1915 . pp:9

Meanwhile back on the western front in the immediate after math of the carnage several hundreds of the men of 137th (Staffordshire) Brigade who had been wounded during the assault on the Hohenzollern Redoubt were being evacuated down the casualty clearing chain to hospitals in France and the United Kingdom.

The War Diary of 1/3rd North Midland Field Ambulance recorded that during the period between the 13th to the 17th October, the unit dealt with 713 casualties at the Advanced Dressing Station in Vermelles.

Private J. Harrison of the 1/5th North Staffords was one of the men treated there:

"At last I arrived at the dressing station, enjoyed some cocoa and chocolate and had my wound attended to, after which I was taken to hospital in a bus, where I partook of some hot milk and bread and butter, and slept a deep sleep until 7 a.m."

Sergeant Sydney Norton, of the 1/6th North Staffords, eventually arrived at a hospital in Devon. From there, he was able to write to his wife in Fazeley and describe how he had reached his present destination:

"I am very comfortable and being well looked after. I only wish they had put me a bit closer to home so you can come and see me but never mind, you will know I am in a safer place and in old England again.

It's a very nice place where I am. About 200 in the same ward and they are all strangers to me. I don't know any of them. It's about 14 miles to Plymouth on the sea coast. I shall be able to tell you more about it next letter.

I arrived here on Sat. night at 6. I started from a place called Bethune in France in a hospital train. It took us 26 hours to get to Le Havre. I was in a bed - nicely fitted up - but in awful pain on my back - could not move. Then I got to No. 2 General Hospital and got my wound dressed before going on the hospital ship. Then we moved on to the ship into beds all fitted up to date. Doctors coming to see us all the while and nurses galore. Then I landed at Southampton and we had to stop in the harbour all night till Sat. morning. We were put into a hospital train there. It took us 10 hours to get to this hospital so you see I had a bit of knocking about. Well, dear, what is putting me about I can't hear no tidings of Caleb and Jack. Has Lisa heard anything? Do let me know for I think all the Tamworth lads got wounded..."

Sapper George Hawkins of 1/2nd North Midland Field Company commented on this in a letter sent from Etretat in France:

"Just a few lines to let you know that I am all right, only still in hospital in a nice little town near the seaside. It is a pleasure to be away from the noise of the guns. It was terrible in that charge. I was buried twice and wounded in the shoulder. People in England do not realise what we have to go through out here."

There was also an improvement in the quality of the food, something that obviously pleased Private John Birch of the 1/5th South Staffords, who was at a hospital in Edinburgh:

"We have eggs for breakfast and chicken for dinner. What a change from bully beef and biscuits!"

Sadly, for some of the wounded Staffordshire men their wounds were so severe that they would prove to be fatal in the following days and weeks.

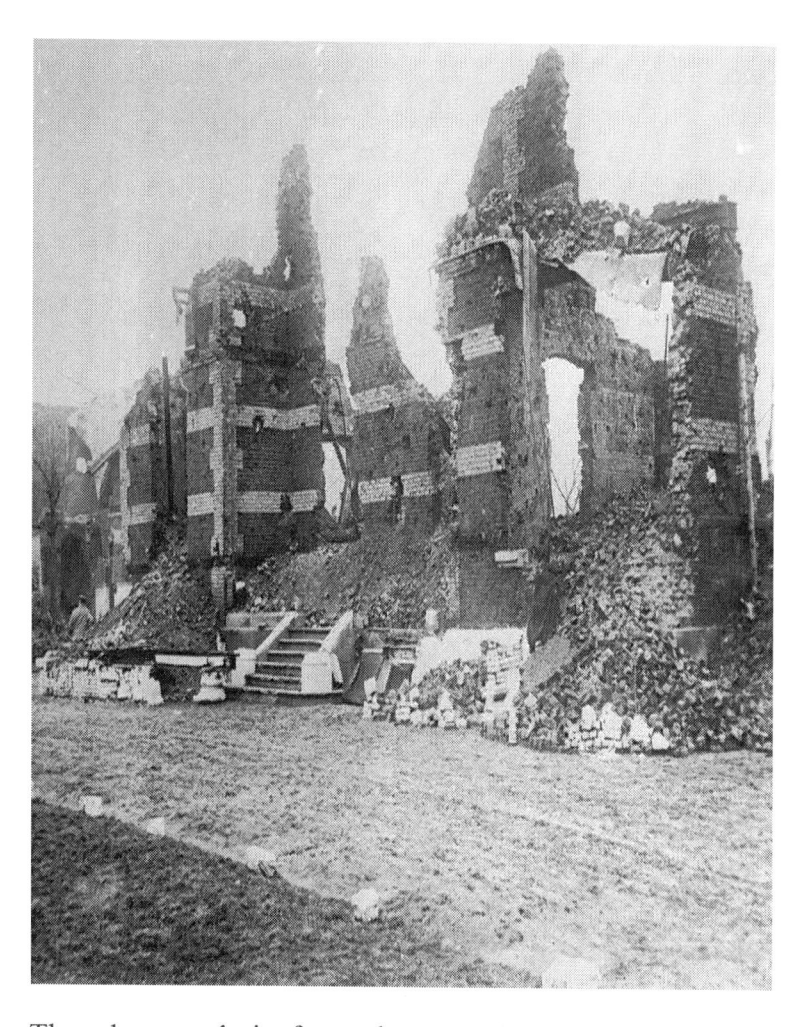

The photograph is from the Imperial War Museum (Q 2227), and is of the ruins of Vermelles Chateau. The Main Dressing Station for 46th (North Midland) Division, set up by 1/3rd North Midland Field Ambulance, was located in the cellars of the ruins.

In conclusion to this chapter the casualties suffered by the infantry were devastating to the communities from which they had been recruited. Several towns in Staffordshire had a large number of casualties as a result of the attack on the

Hohenzollern Redoubt and families were plunged into grief, across the county, from the Black Country in the south to the Potteries in the north, regardless of class and social position.

As the flood of letters began to reach Staffordshire from France, it became evident that the County's Territorial units had experienced shattering losses. The first reports of the attack on the Hohenzollern Redoubt appeared in the local press only eight days after the Brigade had been relieved and, all over the county, pages reacted to accounts of the battle.

"A profound impression has been created in North Staffordshire this week by the news of the heavy casualties among the officers and men of the 1st − 5th North Staffordshire Territorial Regiment, the whole of the county shares in both sorrow and glory on the occasion, for other Regiments of the Division also shared in the success that was achieved and in the losses sustained."

Lord Dartmouth, the Lord Lieutenant of Staffordshire and President of the County Territorial Force Association, wrote regarding the report received from the General Officer commanding the 46th (North Midland) Division:

"The long list of casualties has brought sorrow and mourning to many homes; indeed, the weight of mourning hangs heavy over us all today, but behind it and beyond it stands out the splendid example of courage, sacrifice, and duty, which has been described by those most capable as worthy of the best traditions of the British Army. As a county, then, while we grieve with you in your losses, we rejoice in you in having earned the highest compliments open to a British soldier."

However, news of casualties was only reaching Staffordshire slowly, and the fate of several men was not known. Anxious families besieged the newspaper offices in an attempt to find out what had become of their loved ones. Other families placed appeals in their local newspaper in an attempt to find out what had happened. A few soldiers came home on leave after the action and were questioned by relatives and friends of the missing.38

---

[38] http://www.bfhg.org.uk/Copied-Z-Burntwood-Servicemen-WITTON-Joseph.php

Chapter three:

The fallen men of Staffordshire and the help from present day potters.

One thing when looking up the fallen men, was the sad feeling when during the research, was that these were local men, they lived places I myself knew and what struck me was when brothers came up on the list. Five sets of brothers are known to have died on October 13th 1915, who served in the 1/5th Battalion. There are also two other men, who have not been confirmed as brothers, so could be cousins, their names were 2873 Lance Corporal Reginald Tonks and 2872 Ronald Tonks. It could be assumed they were brothers as they both have consecutive Regimental numbers and both first names begin with the letter R, so it is likely, but has so far not been confirmed that they are brothers.

Five sets of brothers do however have conformation via archives that they were brothers.

2486 Private Alfred Barlow

3699 Private Thomas Barlow

Sons of Matilda Barlow and the late Thomas Barlow, of 30, Meir Hay Road, Normacot, Stoke-on-Trent.

1323 Private Ernest Flannagan,

3478 Private James Flannagan

2075 Private William Flannagan
All three brothers lived in Longton. Sadly this is the only information available of these three brothers.

2207 Private Arthur Glover

1000 Private Graham Glover

Sons of W. G. Glover, who lived at 65, Old Rd in Stone.

3022 Private George Parr

3277 Private Reginald Parr

Sons of Harry and Sarah Ellen Parr, of 56, West Street in Newcastle-under-Lyme.

The Evening Sentinel wrote a small article on these brothers

"we sincerely regret to announce the news that Mr and Mrs Parr of 56 west street Newcastle have received the news that their two sons, Pte George Edward Parr and Pte Reginald Hugh Parr both of the 1/5th Regiment North Staffords were killed in action in France on October 13th. Prior to enlisting, the first named was in the employ of the London and North Western Railway (goods) Longton while the other son formally worked in the electric lighting department."[39]

1550 Private Arthur Dale and 1541 Private Fred Dale, two brother from Kidsgrove, were also killed on 13th October with the 1/5th North Staffords. An obituary notice for Fred Dale appeared in the Sentinel in November 1915.

"Unofficial information was received a few days ago that Private Fred Dale, 1st-5th North Staffordshire Regiment, son of Mr. M. Dale, School-lane, Kidsgrove, was killed in

---

[39] The evening sentinel, November 6th 1915 pp 18

action on October 13th. The parents, however, continued to hope, but on Thursday the suspense was removed by official intimation that he had been killed. Pte. Dale was a member of the 1st-5th North Staffordshire Regiment at the outbreak of the war, and was then mobilised. His brother Arthur was also in the same Regiment, but no tidings of him have been received from him since October 13th. Another brother, Charles, is in a Welsh Regiment and is at present on furlough from France."[40]

It was with the Dale brothers that the most information became available on the Hohenzollern siblings and the only set of brothers who had a photo of them available.

Pte. P. DALE.   Pte. A. DALE.
Killed.   Missing.

---

[40] The evening sentinel november 13th 1915 pp:7

Their parents help on to the hope that Arthur Dale was safe and well, but this was not to be the case. Fred Dale has no known grave and is commemorated on the Loos Memorial, but the body of Arthur Dale was found and identified after the war and is buried in the Canadian Cemetery at Neuville St Vaast, (Plot VIII, Row G, Grave 3)

A Lance corporal who was mentioned earlier was that of Maurice Ewers. In this case Maurice survived the attack, his brother however did not and left this account of his brothers passing.

"My own brother was killed before my eyes. He had gone 200 yards and was getting near the fire trench parapet when a bullet put an end to his life. He fell back into the trench, and was wedged in the bottom. Mercifully, it was almost instantaneous death. I do not know if he instinctively realised that anything was going to happen to him, but he had left his belongings in his valise, and had made out a sort of supplementary will."

One of the rare cases when good news was dealt out was to the father of two young brothers from Burslem. The man to receive this rare good news was a Mr F Boulton, the honorary secretary for soldiers and sailors families association, The Burslem branch. His son's names were B F Boulton and A G Boulton. The Staffordshire evening sentinel wrote the following article in October 1915.

Pte A G Boulton, the younger of the two in a letter date the 17th last refers to the action of the 13th in the following words.

"We had a scrap with the Allamans (Germans) the other day and ended up taking a thousand yards of trenches and a ferocious Redoubt. The price was very great… when the toll was called it was awful, but thank god both Bert and me are in the pink. Our chaps were shot down like sheep, but on we went and hung on like hell until the reinforcements came. My heart jumped for joy when the relief finally came. At the roll call Bert and I were very happy to see each other safe and sound."41

At the foot of the letter was a small message from the other brother saying he was alright. This account has a sense of irony in a way, he speaks so lightly of the attack calling it a scrap, and although it is one of the rare occasions when good news is delivered it is combined with the older brothers sadness and feeling of loss of so many of his fellow Potters.

Some of the youngest soldiers to die in the assault, and whose ages have been confirmed, are commemorated on the memorial.

Pte J. R. RODEY
Killed

---

[41] The evening sentinel, October 23rd 1915 pp: 6

3454 Private Thomas Roden and 3425 Private James Tunstall, who both served with the 1/5th North Staffords, were only 16 years old when they were killed. Private Roden's obituary in the "Staffordshire Weekly Sentinel" reported him as being aged 18 at the time of his death. However, the record provided by the Commonwealth War Graves Commission gives his age as 16. Since his next-of-kin had also provided details to the Commission for inclusion in their records, it could be speculated that Private Roden had lied about his age on enlistment. The youngest known Non-Commissioned Officer to die on 13th October was 8853 Sergeant Thomas Fenton, a Walsall soldier serving with 1/5th South Staffords, who was 19 years old.

The youngest Corporal killed in the assault on the Hohenzollern Redoubt was 3538 Corporal Colonel Willis of the 1/5th North Staffords. Corporal Willis, who came from Longton, was aged seventeen. Corporal colonel Willis was the son of James and Hannah Willis and he was born at 17 Goms mill road, Longton. He appears on two articles in the sentinel that give us some insight into this young man's life. On October 30th 1915 the Staffordshire evening sentinel wrote this regarding young Willis.

"News has been received by Mr and Mrs Willis of 94 stone road Longton that their son corporal Willis 1st 5th North Staffords is missing. Corporal Willis enlisted in October last, prior to that he was employed by Mr James Bourne of Fenton. He was a member the Fenton cricket club."[42]

His parents had an agonizing two month wait to receive the news they must have been dreading.

"Mr and Mrs Willis of 94 stone road, Longton have received news that their son corporal Willis 1st 5th North Staffordshire Regiment has been killed in action. He was reported missing some time ago"[43]

Corporal Willis, Private Roden and Private Tunstall were officially too young to be on active service. All are commemorated on memorials in Stoke on Trent. Corporal Willis is commemorated on both the Longton war memorial and the Minton tile Memorial in the former Fenton Town hall, more recently used as a magistrates court and currently under threat of demolition.

---

[42] The Staffordshire evening sentinel October 30th 1915 pp: 8
[43] The Staffordshire evening sentinel December 18th 1915 pp:4

Corporal Willis, top photo, Longton on the last panel and photo above, the Fenton memorial, second to last name.

Young James Tunstall is the only man who died at Hohenzollern to be commemorated on the Stoke on Trent Railway Station memorial.

Captain Oswald Joseph Bamford

Probably one of the most wealthy and influential men to die during the attack was Captain Oswald Joseph Bamford. He was born into a very influential family that years later would found the company JCB. Bamford had several places he could call his home due to his families wealth, one of which was Alton Castle. His main house was Eaton Lodge. Before joining the army in 1909 he was an engineering manager Messers. He had worked there for 20 years. The website Uttoxeter lost generation has conducted a huge study into Bamford's military career and what follows is from the research they have conducted looking into the history of the 1/6th Battalion of the North Staffordshire Regiment. He was commissioned as a 2nd Lieutenant on March 1st 1909, and became a Lieutenant on March 15th 1913. Bamford went to France in august 1914 and took command of B Company of the 1/6th Battalion of the North Staffordshire Regiment. Through his experience and undying passion to achieve, B Company became one smartest and most skilled in the 1/6th Battalion. By time the war had started he had become Captain and joined the British expeditionary force on October 19th 1914.

Bamford died during the attack during of the Hohenzollern Redoubt. A few minutes before the attack he was seen standing by the parapet, watch in hand saying "steady lads, keep calm". When the attack was due to keep place, Bamford kept too his high standards and led his men over Asif they were on parade, however professional this may have looked, many of his men including himself, were hit by the hail of machine gun fire. His last known words were "come on lads!"

Bamford did not die alone, Lance Corporal James Perkin Fradley, Saw his senior go down and rushed to his aid, sadly Fradley was killed in the attempt to save his life.

A photograph of Fradley who died trying to save Bamford.

Bamford's death cast a Gloomy shadow over the people of Uttoxeter. In a letter to Bamford's father Lieutenant Colonel Radcliff wrote the following.

"I deeply regret to have to convey sad news too you. You will have heard of heavy fighting going on, our troops have been heavily engaged, and I am grieved to say that poor Oswald was one of the killed. Oswald was a brave and plucky officer who did his duty really well. We had to advance against German trenches and were met with fearful rifle and machine gun fire, which laid low so many of our local boys. May I offer my deepest sympathy too you all."[45]

---

[44] http://www.uttoxeterlostgeneration.co.uk/fradleyjp.htm
[45] http://www.uttoxeterlostgeneration.co.uk/bamfordp1.htm

Bamford's body was not found so the people of Uttoxeter had no place to pay their respects to their fallen hero. His father paid for the church where he was a regular member of the congregation, and had a mosaic made in memory of his son, not only that, a stained glass window. Outside in the church yard a cross was erected in his memory. Such dedications were rare for an individual soldier but due to his family's wealth, they could afford such dedications.

DULCE ET DECORUM EST PRO

PATRIA MORI

IN GRATEFUL MEMORY OF

CAPTAIN OSWALD J. BAMFORD

6TH BATT. NORTH STAFFS REGIMENT

SECOND SON OF SAMUEL & DOROTHY BAMFORD

WHO FELL IN ACTION AT LOOS OCT. 13TH 1915

AGED 38 YEARS

REQUIESCAT IN PACE

The dedication left at the base of the cross erected in memory of Captain Oswald Joseph Bamford.

Second Lieutenant Nigel Fyfe Watson Bishop

LIEUT. NIGEL BISHOP
(Killed)

Nigel Fyfe Watson Bishop was the son of Mrs Bishop and Mr James Watson Bishop of Oulton house in Stone. Bishop was educated at Rugby and he worked at Bishop and Stonler pottery firm in Hanley. Bishop volunteered in August 1914 and was commissioned into the 2/5th Battalion in November 1914. The tragic thing for Mr Bishop was the 2/5th Battalion was a relatively safe Battalion to be in. By

January 1915 they had moved to Luton, and then on to St Albans in July 1915. It was in July 1915 he was posted to France to the 1/5th Battalion, which unknowing to him or anyone else would be an almost certain death sentence come October 1915. Had he stayed with the 2/5th Battalion he would have stayed in England until April 1916 to assist in the Easter rising against the British rule of Northern Ireland. Alas that was not to be Bishop's fate, his family received a letter informing them that he had been shot in the head during the final attack and died instantly. He was 23 years old.

Captain Reginald Tavenor Johnson.

1/5th Battalion, the North Staffordshire Regiment.

Reginald Johnson was born in 1879 and was the son of Henry James and Maria Johnson. He grew up at Westwood hall and was educated at Ruby School and Trinity College, Cambridge. On leaving university, Johnson joined the family business, Johnson brothers, which manufactured tableware at several works in the potteries. Johnson was commissioned as a Second-Lieutenant in the 1st Volunteer Battalion, The North Staffordshire Regiment in 1898. He went on active service in South Africa as a member of the

2nd Volunteer Service Company between 1901-02, and earned the Queen's South Africa Medal with three clasps. On his return, he was promoted to Lieutenant but later resigned his commission. Reginald married Margaret Vernon Ford on 1 September 1904 and the couple lived at the Oaklands in Barlaston. At the outbreak of the war, Johnson re-joined his old Battalion, which since the formation of the Territorial Force in April 1908 had been re-titled as the 5th Battalion, and volunteered for Foreign Service overseas. He arrived in France with "B" Company of the 1/5th North Staffords on 3 March 1915. Johnson was promoted to Captain in August 1915 and became the officer commanding "B" Company. On 13th October 1915, Captain Johnson led his company into action at the Hohenzollern Redoubt. One witness described seeing him standing on the parapet of the trench, waving his cane shouting, "Come on, "B" Company!" to encourage his men as they struggled over. He was wounded a few moments later, but was not seen alive again. Reginald Johnson has no known grave and is commemorated on the Loos Memorial. His name can also be found on the Nicholson memorial in leek and war memorial at Barlaston.

There is an article from the evening sentinel dated November 20th 1915, giving details on Captain Johnson's burial.

THE LATE R.T. JOHNSON BURIED WITH TWO OF HIS FELLOW OFFICERS.

"We are informed that the body of captain RT Johnson of the 1/5th North Staffordshire Regiment killed on October 13th at the charge on the Hohenzollern Redoubt was found on the battlefield by a local soldier called Fisher who recognised the officer.

We are now able to publish Private Fisher's letter in which he describes how he found the deceased officer writing to his parents Mr and Mrs T Fisher of Barlaston on November 8th.

I never had such a job in all my life! It was pouring down with rain and about two miles on we got to the front trench which was knee deep in mud, it was grim and I got soaked to the skin.

Yesterday was such a misty morning so I had to walk over the parapet to see if I could find anybody I knew. We were holding the trenches of the 5th North Staffords and we had the job of identification. As I looked who should I find, our captain RT Johnson. I got some papers off him and handed them to an officer of my company. It quite upset me for a time to have found him, perhaps I would have to tell the sad news to Mrs Johnson to console as expected. I have got his cap badge and one of his buttons, perhaps Mrs Johnson would like to have them? He was buried with two other officers."[46]

---

[46] The evening sentinel November 20th 1915 pp:6

Lieutenant Colonel John Hall Knight

One of the most notable men of the 5th North Staffordshire Regiment is Lieutenant Colonel John Hall Knight. He is one of the most documented men of the attack and frequently appears in the Sentinel, both before and after the attack. Knight was born on June 9th 1865 to which the family surname was given to the family business, a solicitors which still exists in Newcastle under Lyme to this very day. The solicitors was founded by his father Joseph in 1840. He was taught to ride horses from an early age and was involved in the hunt with the North Staffordshire Hounds, which were kept at Trentham by the Duke of Sutherland. Knight was educated at Newcastle under Lyme high school and by time he was 15 years old he was being educated at Rugby high school. He lived with the other students at the schools boarding house at 30 Hillmorton road, Rugby. He qualified as a solicitor in 1888. He joined his father and brother at the family firm in 1894. Knight was clerk to Newcastle borough magistrates between 1898 and 1902, and was also secretary of the North Staffordshire Employers Insurance Committee.

Knight married Mary Luxton Jeffrey in 1896 and they settled in Madeley living in Bar Hill house. Their daughter was born in 1902 and they named her Mary Jeffrey Knight. It would appear that knight had an interest in pedigree breeding of cattle. He is listed in the Staffordshire evening Sentinel as having an attractive herd.

Knight's military career began when he Joined the then named 1st Volunteer

Battalion of the North Staffordshire Regiment in 1883. Knight was Promoted Captain in 1889 and made major in 1901. Ultimately he became Lieutenant Colonel and Honorary Colonel of the 1/5th North Staffordshire Territorial Regiment. Knight had an eventful career in the British army. He was assaulted by a man called Thomas Appleby. Appleby had been arrested for obstructing the king's troops. To which the crazed man persisted in wielding around a perambulator (babies pram) in the midst

---

[47] The Staffordshire evening Sentinel, Saturday august 14th 1914.

of the Regiment. Knight saw this disruption to his Regiment dismounted, took the pram off Appleby and told the police to take him away. Knight walked away to inspect his troops, unknowing that Appleby had escaped the grasp of the police man and took a running kick at knight from behind, which injured him rather badly. Appleby was sentenced to one month hard labour in prison. Perhaps his most vivid description of life in the trenches came from a letter he wrote to a Mrs Lovatt.

May 11^h 1915.

"Fortunately the weather has been glorious lately. Now after the Germans are kept under our chief concern is the dead bodies and flies. Of course there are a lot of bodies between the trenches that cannot be touched, we are dealing with the others. The people here before thought that if they put a little lime over the bodies they had done the job nobly. We have done the rest. Inskeep (the Newcastle rural council inspector) would be very useful here.

We are very sorry to lose Geoffrey D yesterday. He was seen when a flare went up and before he could take cover, was hit in front of the trenches. He was very popular especially with the stoke company and they are bursting to avenge him! I am sorry to say we have lost two other men on this tour, Lawrence of B Company and king of C Company. I shall miss them very much."[48]

By October 1915, Knight had become a very much loved and respected man by the men of the 1/5th Battalion. Knight was the first one to leave the Trenches on that fateful day. The Battalion had marched to the British lines the day before, each man issued with three days' rations, 220

---

[48] The Staffordshire evening Sentinel, May 11th 1915.

rounds of ammunition and three empty sandbags. Knight left the trenches, despite knowing the fact that this could be his last day, his riding crop in hand he directed the men towards the Hohenzollern Redoubt. Being in a distinguished uniform, he would have been a noticeable target for the Germans, however it is most probably that because he was in front, and the machine gun fire was so rapid and relentless that it was inevitable he would be one of the first too be hit. The potters carried on towards the Redoubt, falling by the dozen. One private noticed his Lieutenant colonel fall and tried to rescue him. The man was knight's bat man and was named Joseph Mitchell. Despite the onslaught Private Mitchell raced through the bullets to try and help Knight. The Sentinel made this report about Mitchell's heroic act in May 2014.

Throwing him over his shoulder, Private Mitchell climbed out of the ditch that knight was trying to shelter in and turned to begin the journey back to the British lines, to deliver the wounded officer to medics. But amidst the mayhem of the brutal battle, a German sniper picked out the soldier attempting to save the life of his senior officer. The sniper lined up Private Mitchell, aimed carefully and fired. Private Mitchell fell as the sniper's bullet smashed into his right shoulder, passing though his body and exiting out of his lower back. Bleeding and badly wounded, Private Mitchell lost all hope of saving Knight. Despite his wounds, Private Mitchell began a slow and painful crawl back to the British lines. He survived the war and was later awarded the Military Medal for his heroism in trying to rescue Knight.[49]

---

[49] http://www.stokeSentinel.co.uk/Heroic-story-North-Staffords-darkest-days-Great/story-21057555-detail/story.html

Private Joseph Mitchell.

Mitchell's son, Major Albert Mitchell, himself a veteran on the D Day landings that took place in June 1944 has some recollections of his father and the attempt to save knight. He recalls how when he was a young boy, perhaps 13 or 14, when it was approaching Armistice Day his father looked down, he said the reason was he tried to save him but couldn't and admitted to his son that he had failed because he couldn't get him to the medics. This is one of the ways in which we realise how popular Knight was at the time. The Sentinel stated a week after the battle that

Knight was now a household name in Staffordshire. There is a certain sadness, of the fact that Knight was buried without ceremony somewhere close to the battle field, but this location has now been lost. Knight is remembered on the Madeley war memorial and on the Loos memorial in France. Knight was just one of 24 officers killed that day.

Knight was identified by his riding crop, after his body was discovered in early 1916. The Sentinel reported on January 8th 1916

"A party of the 5th Royal Berks buried the body of a full colonel wearing the badge of the North Staffordshire Regiment. When the body was found, a small whip, about two feet in length, bearing the initials MLK was discovered. The whip referred to has been forwarded to Mrs Knight and identified as one belonging to her and used by Colonel Knight. He was an able, careful and soldierly officer and his personal fearlessness was one of his most marked characteristics. He was greatly beloved by his men and how he encouraged them and gave them all the information possible in preparation for the charge."50

Two accounts survive regarding the soldier's feelings towards Knight. Private Joseph Barlow, of Fenton, who was wounded but survived, said:

"The officers sent word along that we were to buck up, that they were proud of us and must bid us a last farewell.

"We raised a cheer and sent word back that we trusted them and were proud of them and would follow them anywhere."

Private R Bruce, who was also wounded, but survived the attack, said in a letter home:

"Our brave colonel led the attack, stick in hand."

---

[50] The Staffordshire evening Sentinel, January 8th 1916.

The final record of knight is when he appears in De Ruvigny's Roll of Honour, 1914-1919.

KNIGHT, JOHN HALL, Lieut.-Col., 5th Battn. The Prince of Wales's (North Staffordshire Regt.) (T.F.), s. of the late Joseph Knight, of Newcastle, Solicitor, b. Newcastle-under-Lyme, co. Stafford, 9 June, 1865; educ. Rugby; was admitted a Solicitor in 1888, and in 1894 joined his father's firm of Solicitors, Messrs. Knight & Sons, Newcastle; subsequently becoming head of the firm after the death of his father, being also Solicitor and Clerk to the Newcastle-under-Lyme Guardians and Secretary to the North Staffordshire Colliery Owners' Association. He joined the 1st Vol. Battn. North Staffordshire Regt. as 2nd Lieut. Aug. 1883; was promoted Lieut., and Capt. 1889, Major 1901, and Lieut.-Col. 15 Dec. 1906, being appointed Hon. Col. Commanding the 1/5th (Territorial) Battn. North Staffordshire Regt.; volunteered for foreign service after the outbreak of war; went to France with his battalion in March, 1915, and was killed in action at the Quarries in the attack on the Hohenzollern Redoubt 13 Oct. following. Buried there on the battle-field. He had the Volunteer Decoration and Coronation Medal, and was mentioned in Despatches by F.M. Sir John (now Lord) French [London Gazette, 1 Jan. 1916], for gallant and distinguished conduct in the field. He was a keen rider to hounds, being a prominent member of the North Staffordshire Hunt, and while at his home at Bar Hill, Madeley, bred hunters. He m. at St. Mark's Church, Hamilton Terrace, London, N.W., 29 July, 1896, Mary Luxton (Bar Hill, Madeley, co. Stafford), only dau. of William Jeffery, and had a dau., Mary Jeffery, b. 15 Feb. 1902.

John Hall Knight.

51

Being 50 years old at the time knight was one of the oldest men to die that day. There had been many successful years of commanding respect and loyalty that he was only too happy to return to his loyal Potters

---

[51] De Ruvingy's roll of honour 1914-1919, volume two page 195.

Lieutenant Colonel Robert Ratcliff

Robert Ratcliff was born in Burton-on-Trent and was educated at Rossall School, before moving on to study at Cambridge University. He was appointed to a directorship at Bass, Ratcliff and Gretton brewery in October 1894, and was the Unionist Member of Parliament for Burton-on-Trent between 1900 and 1918. Ratcliff was commissioned into the 2nd Volunteer Battalion of the North Staffordshire Regiment on 19th March 1887, as a Second-Lieutenant serving with "B" Company at Burton. He was promoted to Lieutenant on 27th July 1889, to Captain on 23rd January 1892, and Major on 18th July 1900. He was appointed an Honorary Lieutenant-Colonel on 21st September 1907, the same year in which he received the Volunteer Decoration. Ratcliff succeeded Lieutenant-Colonel Lord Gretton in command of the 6th North Staffords on 18th November 1909, a post which he held until 26th October 1914. He took over command of the 1/6th North Staffords on 20th May 1915 from Lord Gretton, and remained with the

Battalion until 18th June 1916. When the Territorial Army was reformed in 1921, Ratcliff again assumed command of the 6th North Staffords and also joined the committee of the County Territorial Army Association. He relinquished command of the Battalion in 1924, and retired from the C.T.A.A. the following year. He died in 1943.

In regards to Ratcliff, two interesting letters appeared in the Staffordshire weekly sentinel, which were published on October 27th 1915, and was a correspondence between the Mayor of Burton on Trent and Lieutenant Colonel Ratcliff.

October 20th 1915.

Dear Colonel Ratcliff.

It is with mingled pride and sorrow that Burton has heard of the Gallant action in which the 1/6th North Staffords led by yourself, took part in last week. We are proud that the 6th which in the old volunteer days, was always well spoken of on review days, has more than maintained its reputation as a unit in the Territorial Forces, and now in this time of struggle has shown such splendid soldierly qualities. We are grieved as the news has come through, to heat the death of some and the wounds of many more and would like to express the pride we feel in our Battalion, Our sympathy with the wounded and grief with the fallen. If you can convey to our Burton men the hearty greetings of their fellow citizens at home I shall be grateful.

Yours very faithfully

Jos.S.Rowland.

Lieutenant Colonel Ratcliff felt comforted by the letter and wrote a reply to Mayor Rowland, in which he thanks him but also tries to explain how hard the task was, to which it sounds like Ratcliff felt he had failed despite the Mayors pride.

Dear Mr Mayor.

It was with great pleasure to me to receive your letter of congratulations to the Burton men. They are all indeed splendid, eager to face danger and succeed in the object set us. That we could not do all that was asked of us was no fault of the men of officers who never flinched in the face of a terrible fire from hidden Machine Guns and Rifle fire. After the first few minutes the men had gone forward into the open there were practically no officers left to guide them, and they suffered heavy losses. Then after the attack the acts of bravery and thoughtful help to the wounded were very many. One of the bravest I saw was Drummer boy Clark of Burton. Three times he went over the parapet amidst the bullets to bring back wounded comrades who could not crawl. The first died as he reached the trench, the other two were saved and Drummer Clark was wounded himself and died a few hours later in the trench. , many lying on the floor of the trench frightfully wounded only asked, have we been successful? The Battalion will certainly be glad to receive your kind sympathy.

Believe me, yours sincerely

R.F.Ratcliff- Lt.Col.[52]

---

[52] Both letters from The Staffordshire Weekly Sentinel, Wednesday October 27th 1915. Pp:2.

CAPT. H. A. RIDGWAY
(Killed)

Captain Henry Akroyd Ridgway.

Captain Henry Akroyd Ridgway was a resident of Stone. He was the son of Mr E.A. Ridgway and Mrs .S. Fernie. The sentinel archives mentioned Ridgway twice in 1915, the first describing his lucky written in a letter by Lieutenant Colonel John Hall Knight.

"I am sorry to give you bad news about your boy Raymond. He, Dick and Cpt Ridgway were standing near the railway dugouts about a mile north of Hill 60 at about six in the evening, when a German shell dropped between them. Poor Raymond was killed instantaneously and the Rev Mr Ashby, Chaplain kindly did what he could. Dick had a lucky escape, but is I am afraid wounded by some shell in the shoulder. The doctors attended him very soon, and say it is not dangerous as the joint is un-injured. He will probably be at home, or rather London before you get this letter. He asked me to tell you that Raymond died as he lived, in happiness till the end and knew nothing of the end.

I cannot tell you how sorry how sorry I am to lose Raymond, we were great friends and the Regiment will miss him dreadfully. Ridgway was lucky to escape with a few scratches."53

This is yet again another example of the kind and caring nature of Knight, in the next article titled Captain Ridgway's Bravery, he was not so lucky.

Captain Ridgway's Bravery.

A Private in the Stone Company of the 1st 5th North Staffords who is acting servant to the late Capt Ridgway in writing to his wife sends some vivid details of the recent action.

"We were in the charge on the 13th, I cannot describe it to you, it was in daylight- in the afternoon, and when it started you would have thought you were going into a sham fight. We got over the parapet and then we started to lose men. I had to go over with Capt Ridgway and stick with him. We got close to their first trench, when he got shot and then sent me back for the stretcher bearers, and now I got to them I cannot tell you, it fairly rained bullets and shells. Everywhere you looked you saw them being shot down and the sights were horrible to see but thank God, I got out safe. When I got back to the Captain he had been hit again, by a shell and hit him on forehead besides. I went over to him again and again till I got some men to go over with me at dusk to get him out. Then we had the hard time of carrying him down to the dressing station. We carried him down a trench which took up three or four hours. I never saw a braver soldier and gentleman in my life. I don't know how he bore the pain with the wounds he had, but he stuck it like a Briton and all the other chaps as well. How I came out unscathed I cannot tell as it rained bullets. I was the

---

[53] The Staffordshire weekly Sentinel, August 21st 1915.

only servant out of six who got back. One was killed, four wounded, but Gardiner only slightly. I cannot forget Capt Ridgway. He died about five minutes past eight in the morning."[54]

Captain Ridgway was one of a few men to be buried in a recorded grave. He died aged 30 and is buried in the Loos British Cemetery and his grave reference is XVI.D.13.

Major Edwin W Peach.

Major Edwin W Peach was one of the few men of a higher rank to come out of the attack on the Hohenzollern Redoubt alive. The following article from the sentinel archives gives an insight into his life, views and what happened to him during the battle, part of the article has already been written

---

[54] The Staffordshire weekly Sentinel, October 30th 1915.

earlier in this book, but the following is the whole Sentinel article.

MAJOR E.W.PEACH

Major E W Peach who led the Uttoxeter territorials in the charge was wounded is a son of Mr W H Peach of Westhorpe, Rawley park Stafford and brother of Mr H B Peach of Uttoxeter. Writing home Major Peach says:

"I am wounded in the left thigh, the bone broken above the Knee. I was hit early in the attack while leading my men, of whom I am very proud. They were as cool as if on parade, and charged at quick time. I had a fearfully painful time getting back about 300 yards in the open, crawling with my leg dragging behind, expecting to be hit again every minute. My servant Wilkinson stayed with me like a brick, and lifted up the barbed wire entanglements so that I could get under. Then he bound the leg with two pieces of board to stop it wobbling and carried me on his back for two miles to the Dressing Station, where Colonel Dent set my leg."

Major Peach was sent to Rouen, and afterwards to London. He says the Red Cross organisation is a marvellous system how one gets on every few miles from one hospital to another in France to make room for others coming along and finally shipped to Blighty (the soldier's word for England, derived from an Indian word) is wonderful.

Major Peach is making favourable progress. Major Peach was recently Gazetted temporary Major. He was commissioned as second Lieutenant in the 2nd North Staffordshire Regiment nearly 13 years ago. He served in the South African Campaign. Major Peach got his second station in 1904 and his Captaincy in the 6th Battalion in 1908.[55]

Sergt. H. E. LAWTON.

One man who survived the attack was Sergeant H.E Lawton. His article read as follows in the evening sentinel on December 4th 1915.

GASSED. SEARGENT H.E LAWTON, SILVERDALE

Mrs F Lawton, 4 park road Silverdale has been informed her son Sgt Lawton of the 1/5th North Staffordshire Regiment is in hospital suffering from gas poisoning and shock as a result of the attack on October 13th. Lawton has been in the old volunteer and territorial force for 21 years. After being gassed he was taken to hospital and later brought to England and is in Saint Andrews hospital,

---

[55] The Staffordshire Weekly Sentinel October 30th 1915.

London and doing as well as expected. Lawton was a lieutenant in the Silverdale church lands brigade for 15 years and a bugle major for the territorials for seven years.

Gunner E. MORGAN.

Another man who survived was Gunner E Morgan like Lawton his article appeared in the evening sentinel on December 4th 1915.

INJURED GUNNER ERNEST MORGAN, NEWCASTLE.

Gunner Ernest Morgan who home is at 12 back garden street, Newcastle is in the first Staffordshire battery, RFA but was injured in the gallant assault made by the 1/5th north Staffords on October 13th. Gunner Morgan was one of 16 RFA men who volunteered to go as bomb throwers with the 1/5th north Staffords on October 13th. By the time the charge was made only three of the 16 were left and all three were Newcastle men. Gunner Morgan was badly wounded, another wounded and another gassed. Gunner Morgan who is the son of P.C Morgan of the Newcastle borough police force has been home on sick leave for some time.

Pte. H. DOOLEY.

Another survivor was Private H Dooley, again his article was listed on December 4th 1915.

ILL

PRIVATE H DOOLEY, TUNSTALL

Pte H Dooley whose wife and children live at 59 field street Tunstall enlisted in the 1/5th North Staffords in September 1914 and was part of the push on October 13th last. Since then he has been ill and in hospital in France, but is slowly recovering. Before the war he was working for Messers Peake, Tunstall.

Three of the men missing from the attack were also listed in the Evening Sentinel on December 4th 1915.

Pte. H. ASHMORE.   Pte. F. DOWNING.

MISSING PTES H ASHMORE AND F DOWNING, KIDSGROVE.

News has been received that Pte Harry Ashmore, 1/5th North Staffordshire Regiment son of Mr and Mrs Ashmore, Swan Bank Talke and Pte Frank Downing 1/5th North Staffordshire Regiment , son of MR and Mrs Downing, wellington road, Kidsgrove are reported missing since October 13th. They enlisted together in November last and during the time they have been at the front they have been together. The parents of both soldiers will be glad to receive any news concerning them.

Pte. J. HUMPHRIES.

PRIVATE J.HUMPHRIES, BURSLEM

Mrs Humphries of 78 Dartmouth street, Burslem has received official information that her nephew Pte J Humphries, 1/5th North Staffords has been missing since October 13th. He is an old Sentinel Newsboy.

One man who has a rather tragic story to tell, was actually wounded 10 days before the main attack, on October 3rd 1915, however his story cannot be ignored. Private Thomas James Dale, was wounded by several bullets that smashed into his face, neck and chest, both physically and mentally scaring him whilst in action on the Loos battlefield. The facial wound struck his nose and left him disfigured for life. Dale was being transported home on the day of the attack on October 13th 1915, but with his duty done, he needed to go home to be treated for his wounds.

Private Thomas Dale.

The sentinel published the following article on March 10th 2014.

Thomas, meanwhile, had be sent to the main military hospital at Rouen in France, then taken back to England on the hospital ship Oxfordshire.

He was treated at Chatham in Kent and was able to enjoy some leave with his wife Ethel at home in Longton.

His daughter Annie was born in the summer of 1916.

But despite horrific injuries, the war was not over for Private Dale and he was ordered back to France to re-join his Regiment on January 2nd, 1916.

Throughout the next three years of the war, Private Dale was with the Battalion as it fought in the battles of Albert, High Wood, Poziers Ridge, Ancre, Menin Road Ridge, Poelcapelle and Passchendaele.

However, Thomas did not see out the remainder of the war with his Regiment. On August 6th, 1918, he was sent home, suffering from nose pains and neuralgia, a sudden, severe facial nerve pain that can occur for just a few seconds or last for up to two minutes.

Once home, Thomas was admitted to Chatham Military Hospital, suffering from acute depression, melancholia and an 'epileptic tendency', diagnosed from his time in France.

From Chatham he was sent to East Preston Military Hospital on October 20th, 1918 and then to Brighton Military Hospital a month later.

He finally arrived at the Lord Derby Military Hospital on December 9th, 1918. He never left this final hospital and died on April 20th, 1919, aged 28.

Family historian Dr John Holroyd, has spent many painstaking hours researching the story of his great uncle, Thomas, and has uncovered his medical records.

Longton-born Dr Holroyd, who now lives in Bicester in Oxfordshire – said: Thomas Dale's story is extremely harrowing, but it must be told.

The initial wound in 1915 began to have consequences.

After initial treatment and recovery in late 1915 he began to have 'fits'; minor at first and not sufficient to prevent him from returning to active duty.

However, while the fact that he went back into action a second and third time is testimony to his resilience and fortitude in serving King and country, the number of battles he must have endured, plus the accompanying bombardments and conditions, surely would eventually take its toll.

Throughout his stays at these hospitals and particularly the Lord Derby, his physical demeanour was indicated to be a variable combination of instability, falling over – often in the drill hall – jittery, spasmodic, interspersed with variable onset of epileptic fits. These started in Chatham after his original wound to the face, but became notably established after September 28th, 1918.

He found sleeping difficult and by then suffered from perpetual headaches. He also began displaying uncontrollable shaking of the hands and trembling of the tongue.

Mentally, Thomas was also noted to be depressed by his facial disfigurement from the bullet wound, which apparently had left him with a half-sized squashed nose and a split nasal septum with Rhinorrea (a condition where the nasal cavity fills with mucous). He suffered from acute depression from this and general malaise.

While at the East Preston he was recorded as beginning to have hallucinations and paranoia, thinking that patients were talking and making fun of him, even to the extent of having visions of a funeral party around his bed and that people were suggesting that 'he was certain to die and this was his last day'.

At 6am on November 21th, 1918, while at East Preston he had attempted suicide by cutting his throat with an open razor, resulting in a 6ins wound which, although superficial, indicated his declining condition.

After the wound healed and his transfer to the Lord Derby Hospital, things moderated for a while, before he began having vision problems.

While at Brighton he had been recommended to attend a facial hospital for reconstruction but there is no sign this was ever undertaken.

On February 11th, 1919, he was officially classed as 'insane'. It is sad that such conclusions were reached so readily at the time, compared to the attention and hindsight into mental health that we have today.

Suddenly his eyes began experiencing loss of vision, especially the left. This was diagnosed as optical neuritis, affecting the lens discs. Following potassium iodide treatment, vision appeared to improve and he became more relaxed. He was taken off suicide watch on April 15th, 1919.

Thomas suffered a final massive bout of fits on April 19th, which saw him being put back on the 'dangerous list'.

Despite all attempts, physical and medical, he died at 10.40pm on April 20th, 1919."

Thomas is buried in Longton cemetery, but because he died at the end of the conflict, he is not recognised as a 'war fatality' and does not appear on any of the city's war memorials, or on the Commonwealth War Graves list of the fallen.[56]

As tragic as this article is, there is a bitter sweet victory for Dr Holroyd for the sentinel published a second article on Private Thomas Dale on October 13th 2014, the 99th anniversary of the final attack. The article published in March finished on a sad note that this brave man has never been recognised for his actions, hence he was buried in a civilian grave, not an official Commonwealth War Grave. That has now thankfully been changed due to the ongoing

---

[56] http://www.stokesentinel.co.uk/Traumatic-war-wounds-caused-fits-depression/story-20786671-detail/story.html

efforts to raise awareness of Dr Holroyd's troubled great uncle. The sentinel wrote

The commonwealth war graves commission (CWGC) has agreed to make the grave Longton cemetery a war grave where Private Thomas dale lies.

This must have felt like a great triumph for his decedents, and they hope a War grave to be erected some time in December 2014. Although he is not a casualty of the final attack, this man has a fascinating story, and one of a few, with an almost positive ending, certainly for his family living now anyway.

The men of Fenton.

Fenton has a special connection to the Great War. The Town hall built in 1888 which later became a Magistrates court houses several war memorials. A Mr baker and the Fenton urban district council drew up a deal with the council who brought the town hall for £9,750, equal to around 3/4 million in today's money. One of the memorials is a Minton tile memorial that lists the names of 498 men who fell from Fenton during the Great War. The memorial outside in Albert Square directs the visitor to the town hall memorial with an inscription. The only issue now is you can't enter the building as it is up for sale, much to the worry of the Fenton residents. Alan Gerrard, his wife Cheryl who run an art Gallery in Albert Square and local man Glenn Parkes began a campaign to try and save the town hall from being sold to a private investor, which may lead to its demolition. The large Great War memorial cannot be moved and many residents have relatives on the memorial, such as Jane Jones whose Great Grandfather Ernest Heapy is on the memorial. Many other residents from Fenton and beyond, my self-included ventured down to London to protest about the sale of the building which is owned by the Ministry Of Justice. Our petition with 10,000 names and our campaign gained mass media coverage and support from people such as Stephen Fry. The campaign still continues as the building faces an uncertain future. As for the connection with the Hohenzollern Redoubt, 8 men from Fenton are listed on the memorial, and two more Fenton men who are not. They are as follows.

2060 Sergeant William Baggaley

4020 Private Herbert Charles Brunt

2033 Private Alfred Clayton (not listed on the memorial)

4046 Private Sidney Grainger

2397 Lance Corporal Fredrick Hawley

3600 Private Ernest Hayes

4023 Private George Morgan (not listed on the memorial)

1623 Private John James Walker

192 Company Sergeant Major Henry Washington

3538 Corporal Colonel Willis

The lost men of Uttoxeter.

Uttoxeter, just east of Stoke on Trent famous for the Uttoxeter races was once home to 14 men who fell at the Hohenzollern Redoubt. The most notable was Captain Oswald Joseph Bamford, who has previously been mentioned. The owners of the website uttoxeterlostgeneration.co.uk Alan and Gillian have kindly allowed me to use their information to form this section of the lost men of Uttoxeter.

1823 Private Joseph Blackwell

Joseph does not appear on the 1901 Census, despite the fact that he was born about 1897. A son named William does appear, however, and his date of birth is given as about 1898, which is about right for Joseph. Could Joseph have been called William Joseph, and adopted his middle name when he grew up?

He was a member of the Uttoxeter Territorials before the war. [4]

He was reported missing after the charge on the Hohenzollern Redoubt on the 13th October 1915 and was still missing at the end of December 1915. At the time of his death he was a year under-age for overseas service and should not, therefore, have been there.

2641 Private Henry Bloor

He was wounded in the charge on the Hohenzollern Redoubt on 13th October 1915 and shortly afterwards his parents received a postcard dated 15th October 1915 saying that he had been admitted into hospital wounded and was going on well.

In November 1915 they were still waiting for further news, when rumours reached them that he had died. As no official notification came, they were left very concerned.

They had received a letter from another of their sons who was also serving in the 6th North Staffordshire Regiment, saying that he had not heard anything of his brother Harry and did not know where he was. He added that if ever he got within reach of a German in the future he would have his own back for wounding is brother and cousin. He also expressed deep regret at the loss of his best chum Private Dan Hayes.

They still hadn't received news by the end of December 1915 and posted an appeal for information in the Uttoxeter Advertiser.

They were still waiting for news in the middle of July 1916, by which time he had been missing for nine months. It was not until the end of August that they received official notification of his death.

He left a wife and 3 young children.

1812 Private Harold Curzon

1/6th Battalion, the North Staffordshire Regiment (Territorial Force)

Harold was an only-son and belonged to the local Territorial Company when the war broke out. He lived with his mother at 33, Spiceal Street, Uttoxeter.

He was one of the first of the Uttoxeter men to go to war; he left Uttoxeter with the Uttoxeter contingent of the 1st/6th North Staffordshire Regiment on the 6th of August

1914, just two days after the outbreak of war. . As such, he is counted amongst the special set of men who later became known as the Old Contemptibles.

Given that he was still only 18 when he was killed in October 1915 he will have been only 17 when he first went to the front. The legal minimum age for service abroad at this time was 19. Hence he was not only one of the Old Contemptibles, but also one of Britain's Boy Soldiers.

The Uttoxeter Advertiser said that he was always of a bright and cheerful disposition.

Harold was underage for active service abroad when he took part in the charge on the Hohenzollern Redoubt and went missing. It marked a turning point in the townsfolks attitude to the war, when thoughts that the war was exciting and glorious made way for shock and grief.

In common with so many who died that day, his body was not recovered and he was reported Missing believed killed in November 1915.

He has no known grave and is commemorated on the Loos Memorial for the Missing.

2664 Private James Perkin Fradley.

1/6th Battalion, the North Staffordshire Regiment (Territorial Force)

As a member of the old Volunteer he went through the South African War and on one occasion he was injured when he fell off a wagon.

He was mainly responsible for the formation of the National Reserve at Uttoxeter. He was employed by Messrs. Huggins and Chambers and was 'highly esteemed by his associates.

In the first week of September 1914 the Uttoxeter Advertiser reported that James and a number of other Uttoxeter Reservists had left for war:

Again on Monday the town was agog with excitement; thirteen members of the Uttoxeter detachment of the

National Reserve, who have been certified as fit for active service, leaving the town to join the 6th North Staffs Regiment at Luton.

The veterans assembled at the Cross Keys Hotel yard and headed by the Leighton Ironworks Band and their Commandant, Lieut. Nelson, they marched through cheering crowds to the station to the appropriate strains of where are the Boys of the Old Brigade? The final scenes at the station lacked nothing in the matter of patriotic fervour.

The detachment of National Reserve accepted for service was as follows: Sergt. J. P. Fradley, T. Nield, T. Davies, F. T. Martin, S. H. Whittingham, J. W. Smith, T. Stubbs, A. Smith, J. W. Ford, G. Burrows, J. F. Harrison, W. Lewis and G. Harrison.

Sergt. J. P. Fradley is an old Uttoxeter Volunteer, and was in the South African War. He is the proud possessor of the Queens medal. ...

On the 21st November 1914 it was reported that he had been promoted to Lance-Corporal.

He died in the charge on the Hohenzollern Redoubt at Loos on the 13th of October 1915. He was shot while trying to rescue Oswald Bamford from the battlefield.

Two weeks after the events the Uttoxeter Advertiser described the events leading to James's death.

On Tuesday morning came the news, then unofficial, that Capt. Oswald Bamford had lost his life whilst gallantly leading his men in a charge, and coupled with his name was another well-known townsman in Lance-Corporal James Fradley, who was also reported killed. Unhappily, these reports were later found to be only too true.

But this was not all. Letters arriving in the town continued to report other deaths of Uttoxeter soldiers, and information was also received that more than half the Company had been wounded. Since these reports came to hand, it has been proved beyond doubt that the death-roll has been large, and the most profound impression has been caused throughout the town and district.

It is impossible at present to give exact details of the number of men affected owing to the absence of official information, but the cases dealt with later in these columns give a melancholy idea of how the local Company has suffered, whilst the letters from local soldiers we are able to publish picture in vivid terms the intensity of the battle in which our Territorials were involved.

The fine spirit shown by Capt. Bamford, who has only been in the fighting line about two months, forms the theme of many a communication from the front, and all agree that as a leader Capt. Bamford proved himself an officer of exceptional ability and pluck. .It will be seen that the gallant captain's last words to the brave men he was leading was, Come on lads!

After he fell it is stated that Lance-Corporal J. Fradley went to his assistance, but was himself shot before he could render succour.

James left a wife and two children

In September 1917 it was reported in the Uttoxeter Advertiser that his son, Kenneth James Fradley, had been granted a bursary by the War Pensions Statutory Committee. The bursary was tenable at Thomas Alleyne's Grammar School and had been granted in consideration of his father having nobly laid down his life for his country on October 13th, 1915

1431 Private John (Dan) Hayes

His parents were Mrs. Ada Hayes, of 9, Shaws Yard, Carter Street, Uttoxeter, Staffs.

Before the war he was well-known in local football circles, acting as a trainer to the Uttoxeter Junior Football Club as well as playing himself.

Dan was one of the first contingent of men to leave Uttoxeter upon outbreak of war. He left on 6th August 1914 at the age of 19. This makes him one of the elite band of men known as the Old Contemptibles.

He was a member of the Uttoxeter Territorial Company.

His medal card[3] tells us that he first served in France on 5th March 1915.

He died at the Hohenzollern Redoubt.

On 27th October 1915 the Uttoxeter Advertiser published a letter written by Private Yates stating that he had seen Dan amongst the wounded after the charge on the Hohenzollern Redoubt.

This is not consistent with what was reported in the same newspaper in his obituary[1c], which stated that he was one of the men to jump into the German trench after the charge, and it is thought that he died there.

In November 1915 the Uttoxeter Advertiser reported the fact that Harry Bloor's parents were becoming concerned about the fate of Harry. He had gone missing at the Hohenzollern Redoubt. They had received a letter from another of their sons who was also serving in the 6th North Staffordshire Regiment, saying that he had not heard anything of his brother Harry and did not know where he was. He added that if ever he got within reach of a German in the future he would have his own back for wounding his brother and cousin. He also expressed deep regret at the loss of his best chum Private Dan Hayes.

We do not know which of the Bloor boys this was.

Dan is buried in plot XXVII-L in the Cabaret-Rouge British Cemetery, Souchez.

The "Cabaret Rouge" was a house on the main road about 1 kilometre south of the village of Souchez, near to the site of the cemetery. It is interesting to note that in May 2000 the remains of an unidentified Canadian soldier were

Exhumed from this cemetery and given to Canada so that they could be placed within the Tomb of the Unknown Soldier, in Ottawa.

2673 Private William Harvey Holmes

1/6th Battalion, the North Staffordshire Regiment (Territorial Force)

He was the second son of Fanny Holmes, of 9, Park St., Uttoxeter, Staffordshire, and the late Arthur Holmes.

Thomas Henry Holmes, who also fell, was his brother.

Before the war he was employed at Messrs. Bamford's' works and he was in the old Volunteers[8], having been associated with the Territorials since 1906. Thus, he was one of the Old Contemptibles.

William played for the local Territorials Football Club.

He left the town with the local Company in the autumn of 1914 and left Luton with other recruits for G Company, 1st/6th North Staffordshire Regiment on the 29th of August 1914.

He was killed in the charge on the Hohenzollern Redoubt at Loos.

At the end of October 1915 the Uttoxeter Advertiser published a letter sent to them by Private Yates of the 5th North Staffordshire Regiment. In this letter he said that he had seen William amongst the wounded after the charge. However, in the same issue, the Advertiser also printed a list of local men killed in the charge, and William's name appeared in the list. He was 27 years old.

He has no known grave and is commemorated on the Loos Memorial for the Missing.

2498 Private Herbert Richardson

1/6th Battalion, the North Staffordshire Regiment (Territorial Force)

Before the war he was employed at Messrs. Bamford's and he was as popular in the works as he was in the offices. News of his death was received with the deepest sorrow and regret

His obituary in the Uttoxeter Advertiser stated:

His was a nature one could not help but love and admire. He had an earnest disposition, yet was always full of fun.

So, when his turn came to make history (and what glorious history!) we must be sure that he showed that same quality of fearlessness that was in evidence when engaged in his favourite sport of football, and the same determination with which, when cycling, he tackled the longest journeys or the steepest hills.

It is significant of the present Titanic struggle that both employer and employee should be found fighting side-by-side and falling together. The military training had greatly developed and bronzed young Richardson, and a few months ago, writing home from the base, where he was invalided for a little while, he related that one day when passing an officers tent he saluted the occupant, who evidently did not recognise him. Coming forward, however, the officer asked affably, who are you? And receiving the reply, Bert Richardson, he said, what not Richardson from the office.

Yes, sir.

Well, you have altered said the officer. It was Captain O. J. Bamford, who was then on his way to the trenches. Little did either of them then think that a few weeks hence they would both lay down their lives together in the field of honour.

Bert Richardson was a well-known local pianist and before the war was frequently in demand at local concerts, dances, etc. He was a 'sympathetic player, and gave every promise of making rapid progress in the art.

He was killed in the charge on the Hohenzollern Redoubt at Loos on the 13th of October 1915. He has no known grave and is commemorated on the Loos Memorial.

Private 2121 Arthur George Smith

1/6th Battalion, the North Staffordshire Regiment (Territorial Force)

Almost nothing is known about this man, only he lived at Carter Street, Uttoxeter and that he was listed as missing on October 13th 1915.

2508 Private Sampson Smith

1/6th Battalion, the North Staffordshire Regiment (Territorial Force)

Smith lived in Stone Road in Uttoxeter and joined the local company of territorials after the war was declared and left

Uttoxeter with other recruits on the 29th of August 1914. Not much else is known about Smith other than he fell at Loos leaving behind a wife and two children, however it was reported that Mrs smith received a later from Quarter master Sergeant Copping of the Grenadier Guards said he fell bravely and was laid to rest with some of his comrades. Smith was also mentioned in the memorial service that was held for Captain Bamford. A year later in 1916 his wife posted a memorial notice in the Uttoxeter Advertiser

SMITH:

In loving memory of Sampson smith, who fell in action on October 13th 1915. He rests in the tomb of a warrior's grave, for his king and his country he fought, in heart he was kind, in action he was brave, he has gone to the saviour he sought

From his loving wife and sisters.

They also left a dedication for the second anniversary of his death in 1917.

SMITH:

In loving memory of Pte Sampson smith, killed in action at Hohenzollern Redoubt, October 13th 1915. Some day we hope to meet him, some day we know not when to clasp his hand in that batter land, never to part again

From his loving wife, children and sisters.

2515 Private Sidney Stubbs

1/6th Battalion, the North Staffordshire Regiment (Territorial Force)

Before the war Stubbs was a well-known local pigeon fancier and was a member of the Uttoxeter flying club. In past years he was an enthusiastic pedestrian and won the keeling cup, two years in succession. He was also the possessor of a number of prizes for running. Stubbs was a local territorial and fell during the charge on the Hohenzollern Redoubt and was initially reported missing, later to be presumed dead. He left a wife and child. He had a brother called Charles who was awarded the military medal in 1917.

Private Phillip Bertram Taft (Bertie)

1/6th Battalion, the North Staffordshire Regiment (Territorial Force)

Bertie joined-up in August 1914, which means that he was only 16 years old when he enlisted.

It also means that he was one of the Old Contemptibles.

In September, barely a month after Britain had declared war on Germany, the Uttoxeter Advertiser published an article reporting that Bertram had left with the reservists of Uttoxeter. The article said the following:

The North Staffordshire Railway Station staff at Uttoxeter has been largely depleted through recruiting, both passenger and goods departments having sent their quota. The decision of the men has doubtless been largely influenced by the considerate way in which the Company are treating their employees who join the colours.

On Saturday B. Taft left with the reservists to the Uttoxeter Company of Territorials, and on Monday H. Axon, of the booking office staff, C. Wood, T. Druse and A. Ball left Uttoxeter to join the new Liverpool Regiment which is being raised by Lord Derby..

He was reported as missing immediately after the charge on the Hohenzollern Redoubt at Loos on the 13th October 1915, but it was not until November 1915 that his parents were given official notification of his death.

According to his obituary in the Uttoxeter advertiser he was a courteous lad who was to be sadly missed by all who knew him. He had an older brother, Lance Corporal Richard H Taft who was serving in the 5th queens Regiment in India when his brother was killed.

2994 Private William Tyson
1/6th Battalion, The North Staffordshire Regiment
(Territorial Force)

William Tyson was born in 1895 and lived with his widowed mother at 31 The Hockley in Uttoxeter. Before the war, William had worked as a gardener and had been employed by Mr A.C. Bunting and John Bamford. He had enlisted in the 6th Battalion, The North Staffords at Uttoxeter on 2nd September 1914 and landed in France with "C" Company of the 1/6th North Staffords in March 1915.

Private Tyson was killed in action at the Hohenzollern Redoubt on 13th October 1915. His body was recovered by soldiers of the Guards Division and Company-Quartermaster-Sergeant Copping of the Grenadier Guards wrote to Mrs Tyson to inform her that they had buried her son:

"Just a line to tell you the sad news that I buried Private Tyson, who was killed in action fighting for his King and Country. He fell in battle like a British hero, and we buried him with some more of his gallant comrades. I hope you will bear the news with a stout heart."

The location of William's grave was lost and he is therefore commemorated on the Loos Memorial. The Information on William Tyson was kindly supplied by Andrew Thornton via Facebook

Before we move on to those present day potters who helped with this book, I think it is important to briefly look at those who fell under the Banner of the North Staffordshire Regiment who were not born in Staffordshire and the potteries.

1/5th Battalion North Staffordshire Regiment:

Private 2233 Harrold Breeze born in Leeds, Enlisted in Tunstall.

Company Quarter Master Sergeant George Algernon Couzens, Born in Chelsea, Enlisted in Hanley, lived in Stone.

Private 3018 Thomas Gilbert, born Nuneaton, Warwickshire, Enlisted in Shelton.

Private Nathan Goodrum born Downham Market, Norfolk, Enlisted in Hanley.

Private 2817 Ashworth Gough born Coalport, Salop, Shropshire, Enlisted Hanley.

Private 1547 William Greenhough, Born Manchester, Enlisted in Tunstall.

Private 2641 Oliver Hugh Griffith born Bangor, Carnarvon, enlisted inTunstall.

Private 3872 Gordon Clarence Leckie, born Liverpool Enlisted in Shelton.

Lieutenant Sergeant Arnold Lewis, born Barbados, Enlisted in Biddulph.

Private 3146 Duncan Mclarance, born Newcastle upon Tyne, Enlisted in Shelton.

Private 3251 Christopher Mitford, born Alsager Cheshire, Enlisted in Hanley

Private 2600 William Muston, born Alsager Cheshire, Enlisted in Newcastle under Lyme.

Private 3280 John Perks, born Worfield Salop, Shropshire, Enlisted in Stoke.

Lance Corporal David Robinson, born Oldham Lancashire, Enlisted in Biddulph

Private 2700 William Thomas Sherry, Born Nottingham, Enlisted in Hanley.

Private 1575 James Smith born Tutbury, Derbyshire, and Enlisted in Stone.

Private 3733 James Townsend, born Dudley, Worcestershire, Enlisted in Shelton.

Sergeant 1522 Walter Washbrook, born Oxford, Enlisted in Tunstall.

Lance Corporal John Whitehouse, born Dudley, Worcestershire, Enlisted in Newcastle under Lyme.

Private 3192 Charles John Wilson, born Tutbury Derbyshire, Enlisted in Shelton.

The Variation in the 1/6th Battalion of the North Staffordshire Regiment is less varied, the base was in Burton on Trent, which is where the vast majority came from and they like everyone else will appear on the Roll of Honour. Those not from Staffordshire in the 1/6th Battalion were as follows.

Sergeant George Cutler, born Saint Pancras, Middlesex, Enlisted in Burton on Trent.

Private 1812 Harold Curzon, born Oldham Lancashire, Enlisted in Uttoxeter

Private 3607 Henry William Gent, born Woodvile Derbyshire, Enlisted in Burton on Trent

Private 2470 Thomas Wells Hallam, born Beccles, Suffolk, Enlisted in Burton on Trent.

Private 3099 Joseph Jevons born Northampton, Enlisted in Burton on Trent.

Private 3039 John Francis Kelham, born Huggelscote, Leicestershire, enlisted in Burton on Trent.

Private 1818 Norman Lomas born Tideswell Derbyshire, enlisted in Burton on Trent.

Private 1988 Frank Marsh born Birmingham, enlisted in Tamworth, lived in Burton on Trent.

Private 2375 Ernest Lewis Plumb born Hendon Middlesex, enlisted in Burton on Trent.

Private 2121 Arthur George Smith born Doveridge Derbyshire, enlisted in Uttoxeter.

Private 2187 William Albert Stockwell born Cirencester, Gloucestershire, enlisted in Burton on Trent.

Private 1953 Joseph Harold Wainwright born Kettlebrook, Warwickshire, enlisted in Tamworth, lived in Burton on Trent

Help from present day Potters

In progressing with the book, I thought it would be wise to make a public appeal to the people living in Staffordshire today. I saw an advertisement in the sentinel asking for anyone who had relatives who served in the Great War to come forward. I sent an email to the editor of the section of the newspaper, which is called the way we were. The editor Colette Warbrook, happily agreed to help and published my article accompanied by images of the Hohenzollern Redoubt and Lieutenant Colonel John Hall Knight.

"Imagine the scene.

October 13th 1915. The last day of the Battle of Loos.

Thousands of men, waiting for that signal, the sharp blast of the whistle.

The pocket watch strikes two and over they go, led by Lieutenant Colonel John Hall Knight, of Newcastle-under-Lyme, directing the men with his riding crop towards the almost impenetrable fortress known as the Hohenzollern Redoubt.

What followed was a massacre. More than 3,600 fell in one hour.

Seven hundred of the men who went over the top that day called Stoke-on-Trent their home.

Five hundred fell. They died with Stoke-on-Trent in their hearts, and in our hearts they shall remain.

I am in the process of writing a book about that fateful day in 1915, focusing mostly on the 5th Battalion of the North Staffordshire Regiment, but also the 6th Battalion, who called Burton on Trent, Leek and Uttoxeter their home.

The 5th being mostly residents of Stoke-on-Trent.

I'm compiling a list of the fallen and trying to use relevant documents and photographs.

The book will be an in-depth look at the battle from the Staffordshire point of view.

If any readers are related to men who fell or who survived at the Hohenzollern Redoubt battle on October 13th, 1915, please get in touch.

I'd also like to hear from people who have information regarding the attack.

People will, of course, be credited in the book.

CALLAN CHEVIN Blurton"

Then the waiting began, however it became apparent that people were still interested because in just over three weeks I got approximately two dozen replies, both via Email and via my mobile phone.

The first to contact me was a Mrs Trixie Bennett, born in 1936 of Smallthorne, Near Burslem. Trixie called me on my mobile and told me of her relative, 2097 Private William Henry Shaw. William was listed as being 18 years old at the time of the attack on Hohenzollern, and enlisted 2 years before aged just. There was three sisters and two brothers and Trixie explained that Private Shaw joined to earn some money for his family because both of their parents Thomas and Ann Shaw had passed away, leaving young William alone to bring up his younger siblings. The family lived at 3 Adelaide Street in Burslem, Stoke on Trent.

In contrast to my idea, Trixie had also sent a letter she wanted to be published in the sentinel's, the way we were.

"My uncle, William Henry Shaw, from Adelaide Street, Burslem, was killed during the First World War on October 13, 1915.

He had joined the Army at the age of 16, and died aged 18 at Loos. His name was on a memorial at Moorland Road School, but I'm not sure where it is now. Can anyone help me locate it?

TRIXIE BENNETT Smallthorne"[57]

In Trixie's conversation to me she mentioned this memorial, so I decided to search for her on the sentinel website and found her story online. There are two memorials in Cobridge, Stoke on Trent. One lists 120 men who fell from the Cobridge area, the other memorial listing 69 men of the North Road area of Cobridge. The sentinel reported in January 2014,

"Pensioner Trixie Bennett launched a campaign to save the memorial after concerns were raised it could be lost after its former home, Bennett's Tavern off North Road, was sold at auction to make way for housing.

---

[57] http://www.stokesentinel.co.uk/Way-World-War-1-memorial/story-20587067-detail/story.html

The 77-year-old, of Bramley Road, Smallthorne, who used to run the pub with husband, Fred, for 15 years during the 1970s and 80s, said: "I was really glad when the memorial was finally relocated to the church because it was something that kept playing on my mind constantly.

When it was closed, I used to walk past the pub to see if the memorial was still there.

"I thought it was a great idea when a member of the church called me to say they thinking of setting up a committee to organise events to honour the men named on the two plaques inside the church.

"My uncle William Henry Shaw died in October 1915 at the age of 18 while serving in the war.

His name used to be on a plaque located in Moorland Road High School in Burslem and I used to visit it on the Friday before Remembrance Sunday every year. It is still very important to me that we remember all the young soldiers who died in the war."[58]

The plaque from the closed pub, Bennett's Tavern was removed and rehomed at Christ church in Cobridge in April 2014.

---

[58] http://www.stokesentinel.co.uk/Parishioners-Cobridge-church-launch-campaign/story-20443211-detail/story.html

59

Trixie Bennett and the memorial plaque, in its new home. Following Trixie's successful memorial campaign she is now involved in trying to keep her home town of Smallthorne litter free and free from anti-social behaviour.

---

[59] http://www.stokesentinel.co.uk/War-tribute-unveiled-Christ-Church-Cobridge-video/story-18778662-detail/story.html

Elaine Clayton sent me the following email, the first I received, the day my Article was published.

Hello Callan

I am most interested in the book you are compiling here is a photo of William Edward fletcher who died on this day he was my husband's great uncle he was from Burslem and the sentinel picture which I found good luck with your book best wishes Elaine clayton.

The email was accompanied by the following photograph of her Husband's Great Uncle.

On the same day I received an email from a Lynn Ormston.

"Callan,

Regarding your article in tonight's sentinel regarding Hohenzollern Redoubt battle, my grandma's first husband was killed in that battle, 13/10/1915. He was William Thomas Sherry aged 22, he was born in Nottingham in 1892, son of Thomas William and Lucy Sherry, my grandma was Agnes Eldershaw, they married 1912 and had 3 children, the last one he never saw. He was in 1st/5th North Staffordshire Regiment, number 2700, he is buried at Pas De Calais, France, Loos Memorial, and I have his Army papers and photos of him if you're interested.

Regards Lynn"

Obviously interested I thanked and requested for the extra information to be sent to me.

Lynn sent me a wealth of information in the form of documents and a photo of her Grandma and besides her husband.

From the documents kindly sent to me it is possible to recreate this man's brief history in the North Staffordshire Regiment.

Army Form E. 50

TERRITORIAL FORCE.
(One year's Embodied Service at Home).
ATTESTATION OF

No. _____ Name William Thomas Sherry Corps 5th N. Stafford Regt

Questions to be put to the Man before Enlistment

1. What is your Name? — 1. William Thomas Sherry
2. In or near what Parish or Town were you born? — 2. In the Parish of Wolverhampton in or near the Town of Wolverhampton in the County of Staffs
3. Are you a British Subject? — 3. Yes
4. What is your Age? — 4. 18 years ___ Months.
5. What is your Trade or Calling? — 5. Miner
6. Have you resided out of your Father's house for three years continuously in the same place, or occupied a house or land of the yearly value of £10 for one year, and paid rates for the same, and, in either case, if so, state where? — 6. No

You are hereby warned that if after enlistment it is found that you have given a wilfully false answer to any of the following seven questions, you will be liable to a punishment of two years' imprisonment with hard labour.

7. Are you Married? — 7. No
8. Have you ever been sentenced to Imprisonment by the Civil Power? — 8. No
9. Do you now belong to the Royal Navy, the Army, the Royal Marines, the Militia, the Special Reserve, the Territorial Force, the Army Reserve, the Militia Reserve, or any Naval Reserve Force? If so, to what unit and Corps? — 9. No
10. Have you ever served in the Royal Navy, the Army, the Royal Marines, the Militia, the Special Reserve, the Territorial Force, the Imperial Yeomanry, the Volunteers, the Army Reserve, the Militia Reserve, or any Naval Reserve Force? If so, state which unit, and cause of discharge. — 10. ___
11. Have you truly stated the whole of your previous Service? — 11. Yes
12. Have you ever been rejected or discharged as unfit for the Military or Naval Forces of the Crown? If so, on what grounds? — 12. No
13. Are you willing to be vaccinated or re-vaccinated? — 13. Yes
14. Did you receive a Notice, and do you understand its meaning, and who gave it to you? — 14. Yes { Name ___ Sherry Corps 5 N. S. Regt }
15. Are you willing to serve in the United Kingdom upon the following conditions provided His Majesty should so long require your services:— ... — 15. Yes

I, William Thomas Sherry, do solemnly declare that the above answers made by me to the above questions are true, and that I am willing to fulfil the engagements made.

William Thomas Sherry SIGNATURE OF MAN.
William Leigh Signature of Witness.

OATH TO BE TAKEN BY MAN ON ATTESTATION.

I, William Thomas Sherry, swear by Almighty God, that I will be faithful and bear true Allegiance to His Majesty King George the Fifth, His Heirs, and Successors, and that I will, as in duty bound, honestly and faithfully defend His Majesty, His Heirs, and Successors, in Person, Crown, and Dignity against all enemies, and will observe and obey all orders of His Majesty, His Heirs, and Successors, and of the Generals and Officers set over me. So help me God.

CERTIFICATE OF MAGISTRATE OR ATTESTING OFFICER.

The above-named Man was cautioned by me that if he made any false answer to any of the above questions he would be liable to be punished as provided in the Army Act.
The questions were then read to the Man in my presence.
I have taken care that he understands each question, and that his answer to each question has been duly entered as replied to, and the said man has made and signed the declaration and taken the oath before me at ___ on this 21st day of August 1914

Signature of the Justice ___

The Attestation form of William Thomas sherry reveals he previously served with the North Staffordshire Regiment. The Article is dated 27th August 1914, and includes the Oath to his allegiance to His majesty King George V.

"I William Thomas Sherry swear by almighty god, that I will be faithful and bear true allegiance to His Majesty King George the fifth, his Heirs and Successors, and that I will in duty bound, honestly and faithfully defend his Majesty, his Heirs and Successors, in Person Crown and dignity against all enemies will observe and obey all orders of his Majesty, his Heirs and Successors and of the Generals and Officers set above me. So help me God."

The following articles are interesting as they show what would happen to the family of a fallen soldier, and that the process was a lengthy one, which at the time must have been distressing for Agnes and her children, as right up until 1920, they were being reminded of his death, but in the present times, we know how many men fell, during the Great War and that the process of awarding pensions and delivering the correct medals was at the time an amazing fete of organisational skills.

Effects—Form 118A.

MEMORANDUM FOR

The Officer in charge of _____ Records.

WAR OFFICE,
IMPERIAL INSTITUTE,
SOUTH KENSINGTON,
LONDON, S.W.7.

_____ 191_

Will you please note any articles of personal property now in your possession or subsequently received by you belonging to the late _____
_____
should be despatched to :—
_____
_____
_____
_____

Any medals granted to the deceased that are now in your possession or that may hereafter reach you should be disposed of to :—
_____

C. Harris
Assistant Financial Secretary.

In this article dated October 24th 1915, we see the memorandum, give responsibility given to Harris, an Assistant financial secretary, for Sherry's belongings and any potential medals to be successfully delivered to Williams's wife, Agnes. The next article was date March 17th 1916, and stated that the belongings of Private sherry were now his Harris's possession, following this the next article was dated July 3rd 1916 and shows the conformation that Agnes has received a pension to support her family after the loss of Private Sherry.

(8 1 9) W 334—583 5203 4/15 H W V(P 76)(5)
    11395—1671 20,000 11/15

MEMORANDUM FOR

The Officer in charge of

Y. F. Records,

Lichfield

[Stamp: TERRITORIAL FORCE RECORDS 17 MAR 1916]

Effects—Form 118A.

Any further communication on this subject should be addressed to:—
The Secretary,
War Office,
Park Buildings,
St. James's Park,
London, S.W.,
and the following number quoted.

WAR OFFICE,
PARK BUILDINGS,
ST. JAMES'S PARK,
LONDON, S.W.,
14th March 1916.

E. 1/50210/1 (Accounts 4.)

Will you please note that any articles of personal property now in your possession belonging to the late No. 2700 Private William Thomas Cherry, 1/5th Bn. North Staffordshire Regt. should be despatched to:—

Mrs Agnes Cherry
1, Pleasant Row
Hack Lane
Trent Vale
Stoke-on-Trent

Any medals granted to the deceased that are now in your possession or that may hereafter reach you should be forwarded to:—

Same person

C. Harris
Assistant Financial Secretary.

F. 3.—Form 50b.

WAR OFFICE,
LONDON, S.W.,

Any further communication on this subject should be addressed to—
The Secretary,
War Office,
London, S.W.,
and the following number quoted.

3rd July 1916

No. 280 n. Staff (F. 3.)

Sir,

I am directed to inform you that the widow of No. 2700 Pte. Wm Thos Sherry 5th North Staffordshire Regt. has been awarded a Pension of 20/6 a week, for herself and three children, with effect from the 10-7-16.

The Officer issuing Separation Allowance has been informed of the Award.

The Pension will be paid from the Central Army Pension Issue Office.

The certificates received in support of the application have been returned to the widow.

I am, Sir,

Your obedient Servant,

C. Harris

Assistant Financial Secretary.

T. F.
Officer in charge of Records,
Lichfield.

The final two documents date from 1919 and 1921, and are the certificates that would have been sent to William's wife Agnes in recognition of his service and sacrifice and show her receiving his medals.

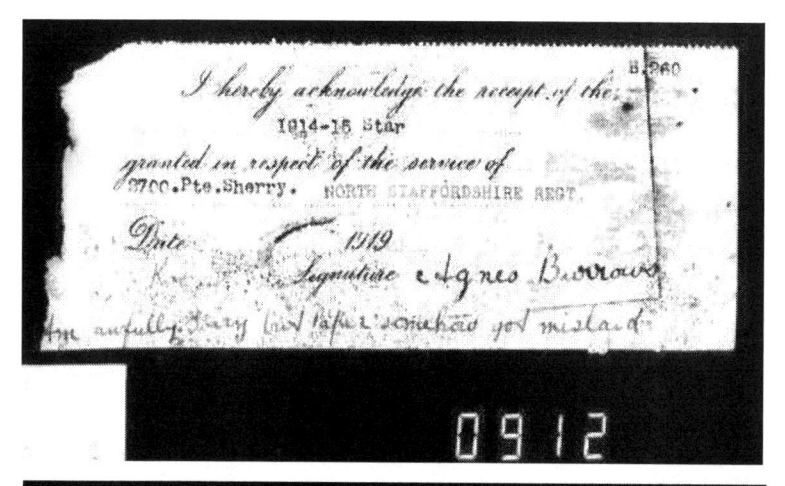

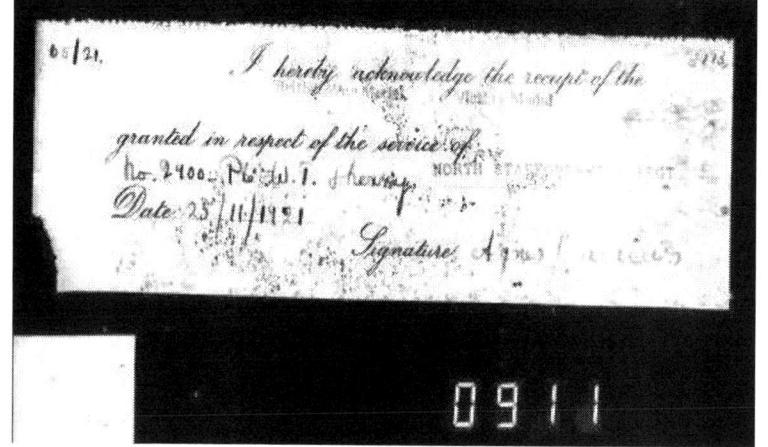

In relation to those who fell and left their greiving families behind, this rather chilling article from the evening sentinel, shows the faces of just a handful of women from the potteires, who lost a husband, son, brother or cousin that day.

PHOTOGRAPHS PICKED UP ON THE FIELD OF BATTLE.

Photographs of which the above are copies, were picked up on the battlefield near Hulluch in France, by Corpl Mohama of the 2nd Scots Guards, who found an address in the Potteries on the back of another not included in the above to which he sent the lot. On one is the name of a private of the 1st or 2nd North Staffords. The portrait of the lady we published last week has been identified, and the photograph handed over.

60

The caption reads, photographs of wich the above copies were picked up on the battlefield near Hulluch in france by corporal mohema of the 2nd scotts Guards, who found an address in the potteies on the back of another, not included in the above to which he sent the lot. The portrait of the lady last week has been identified and handed over.

What this article basicaly is is an suggestive advertisiment, hoping to not only give back the photos to the ladies, but also a way of identifying who was killed in the attack.

---

[60] The evening sentinel, November 27th 1915 pp:6

FROM THE BATTLEFIELD

This is the photograph that was succsefuly handed over to the lady in the photograph. From the letter on the back, it was gathered she was a sister of a man called Leonard and her name was Edith.

---

[61] The evening sentinel, November 20th 1915 pp:6

Back to the emails I Received on October 5th 2014 came from Susan Lawton.

Dear Callan,
As I opened the page in the Sentinel, the photograph of Colonel Knight made me go quite funny!! I recognised his face. It took my mind back about 40 years when I was at High school, I did a project on Col. Knight and the 5th North Staffs. I had forgotten about it until I read your letter, but knew I still had it somewhere in the house, because I love my local history I saved it. I have found the project. I would love to help with your book, if I can help at all please get in touch.
Sue Lawton

The day after I received an Email from Sue Giles of Eccleshall.

Dear Callan
In reply to your letter in the Sentinel on Saturday, my uncle died on 13th October 1915 at the Battle of Loos. He lived in Woore but was with
the 5th North Staffs and became a Lance Corporal. His name was Joseph Collin Brown and his number was 3307. I have a copy of the form he signed when he joined up and a copy of the notification when he was killed in action. His grave/memorial ref is 103 to 105 Loos Memorial.
I hope this will be of use to you.
Yours sincerely
Sue Giles
Not long after Sue sent me a photograph of a man in uniform she believed was her First World War relative.

I needed some help on this photograph, I was certain it was a second world war soldier, and after consulting Andrew Thornton and other Administrators of various military themed pages on Facebook, we all come to the conclusion that this was not Joseph Collin brown who died at Loos, but possibly a younger relative, a nephew possibly. Sue had come to the conclusion that this was the end of my study in to her relative, however, I knew somewhere where they may have been a photograph, the sentinel Archives. I did a general search and found a Private JC Brown. I sent the newspaper image to Sue explaining don't worry that he is listed as a Private because the photo would have been taken when he was a private and with so many deaths in such a short space of time, updating the ranks would not have been top priority, just simply recording and publishing the deaths was. Mrs Sue Giles was very happy with the image and emailed me back thanking me for taking the time to look for her relative.

Pte. T. C. BROWN
killed

On the 99th anniversary of the attack I received an email from a Mr Paul Dyer.

"Hi Callan,
My Great Uncle was killed on 13 October 1915, 99 years ago today whilst attacking the Hohenzollern Redoubt.
He was a member of the Leicestershire Regiment who went over the top the same time as the other Regiments on that fateful day.
I have been to the Hohenzollern Redoubt many times over the last ten years, and I know the ground extremely well.
I have digitally overlaid modern maps with the original trench maps, and I have been able to walk at the exact locations of the original trench lines and identify the exact

locations where each Regiment stood prior to going over the top.
See attached for a photo I took of the Redoubt from the British trench line.
Have you managed to get across to France and visit it yet?
Regards,
Paul."

In reply to my email he told me he could not supply the maps as he did not own copyright over the images, however did give me some good advice if I ever intended to travel to the sight of the battle.

"Don't wait until next year to go over, go a few times before then. Winter is good because the vegetation has shrunk back exposing the lie of the land, especially inside the redoubt, as there is a massive crater inside that is completely hidden by vegetation. Summer is also good because it's warmer and the days are longer, but the vegetation can be overgrown.
See the attached photos, you can just about make out the shape of the crater through all the vegetation.
It is easy to get across to visit. Day trips are easy using the Channel Tunnel and you would get at least 9 hours if you wanted on location.
Regards,
Paul."

On October 4th 2014, I received the following text on my mobile phone from a Mr Trevor Davenhill.

"Regarding your enq in today's sentinel I have a distant relative killed at the Hohenzollern Redoubt. He is lance corp 2850 of the 1st 5th North Staffs Reg territorial forces, served in no 4 plat of a comp. he was killed on that date during the assault by the 46th north mid division. Body not identified, was commemorated on Loos memorial and men at Granville Sq at Stone. Trevor Davenhill."

A curious thing about this was I recognised the name, Davenhill. I had seen his photograph in the sentinel archives, I was sure of it. After a conversation via phone and several texts later we confirmed the photo was of his relative. It is quite rare in this case that somebody has the same name as one of the fallen as so many were killed and so many were young and had not yet had children. Trevor did not know how he was related, but asked me if he could have his relatives photograph, so I asked Andrew Thornton if he knew anything about this man, Lance Corporal Frank Davenhill, and from his information I was able to make the following page in dedication of Frank.

Pte. F. DAVENHILL

KILLED
5TH NORTH STAFFORDS (1 I)

Allen 2818 Corporal G
Alletton 2918 Sergeant C B
Baggilly 2369 Private G W
Bailey 3399 Private T
Bond 2173 Lance Corporal L.
Brett 2076 Private S
Brown 3989 Private J C
Casey, 3938 Private J
Clare 1705 Private A
Cope 2678 Lance Corporal G
Cousens 2811 Coy Quartermaster Sergt A G
Dale 15-1 Private T
Davenhill 2850 Lance Corporal F

2850   Lance-Corporal   Frank   Davenhill 1/5th Battalion, The North Staffordshire Regiment (Territorial Force)

Frank Davenhill was born in Stone and lived at Whitebridge in the town. His parents resided at Meaford Crossing, where his father was employed as a signalman by the North Staffordshire Railway. Before enlisted shortly after the outbreak of the war, Frank had worked at Haynes and Sons wheelwrights at Station Road in Stone. Lance-Corporal Davenhill served with No. 4 Platoon of "A" Company. He was killed in action on 13th October 1915 during the assault of the Hohenzollern Redoubt by 46th (North Midland) Division. His body was not identified after the war and he is commemorated on the Loos Memorial. He is also remembered on the war memorial at Granville Square in Stone.

One email that I received I found particularly humbled and honoured that this lady had taken the time to email me, the reason being is because she is 95 years old, and the niece of one of the fallen who fell on October 13th 1915. The lady requested that she not be named in the book but was kind enough to give me some photographs and a poem written by her Father about his brother.

"Hi, I hope this email comes to you OK. My age is 95 and eyesight not good, my uncle private George Coomer was killed in the Battle of Loos.eg Private George Coomer of Newcastle under Lyme age 21 Reg number 3623. His name is right at the top of a column at Duds Corner cemetery, my son Peter has some details and a photo and 'shield' as was given to all relatives of the dead. As a child I was encouraged to honour and remember him, my favourite hymn was .O Valiant hearts, and my father painted an illuminated address in memory of uncle George; it was a treasured reminder of him when we visited grandparents.(How sleep the brave who sink to rest etc. My niece has it now, I have a rough copy if you would be interested over the years it has faded but still a beautiful memory, I find there is lot of information on a site worked by Andrew Thornton."

Private George Coomer, standing on the left with his family.

Another email the lady sent me was as follows.

"Further to our last communication I am attaching a picture of an illuminated script written by my Father, William Coomer. This was written in memory of his brother George who was killed in the Battle of Loos, WW1.

The quality of this, I'm afraid, is very poor. The wording is taken from a poem, a transcript is given as follows"

HOW sleep the brave, who sink to rest

by all their country's wishes blest!

When spring, with dewy fingers cold,

Returns to deck their hallowed mould,

She there shall dress a sweeter sod

Than Fancy's feet have ever trod.

By fairy hands their knell is rung;

by forms unseen their dirge is sung;

There Honour comes, a pilgrim grey,

To bless the turf that wraps their clay;

And Freedom shall awhile repair

To dwell, a weeping hermit, there!

In relation to those who fell and left their greiving families behind, this rather chilling article from the evening sentinel, shows the faces of just a handful of women from the potteires, who lost a husband, son, brother or cousin that day.

PHOTOGRAPHS PICKED UP ON THE FIELD OF BATTLE.

Photographs of which the above are copies, were picked up on the battlefield near Hulluch in France, by Corpl Mehuma of the 2nd Scots Guards, who found an address in the Potteries on the back of another not included in the above to which he sent the lot. On one is the name of a nurse of the 1st of 3rd North Staffords. The portrait of the lady we published last week has been identified, and the photograph handed over.

The caption reads, photographs of wich the above copies were picked up on the battlefield near Hulluch in france by corporal mohema of the 2nd scotts Guards, who found an address in the potteies on the back of another, not included in the above to which he sent the lot. The portrait of the lady last week has been identified and handed over. What this article basicaly is is an suggestive advertisiment, hoping to not only give back the photos to the ladies, but also a way of identifying who was killed in the attack.

On november 3rd 2014, I recived a handwritten letter, with a document enclosed that resembled a post card, and the creator was a Mr Phil Rowley, who works at williamson's photographic shop in Gold street longton. He also enclosed the poem by Charles Hamilton Sorley. Mr Rowley informed me that Sorley was born in Aberdeen in 1895 and was educated at Malborough college. At the out break of war he was due to go and study at Oxford university, but decided to serve his country, and joined the 7th Battalion of the Suffolk Regiement. Charles Hamiilton Sorley was

232 | Page

killed in action on October 13th 1915, at the Hohenzollern Redoubt, and this was the poem enclosed.

WHEN YOU SEE MILLIONS OF THE MOUTHLESS DEAD

When you see millions of the mouthless dead
across your dreams in pale Battalions go,
Say not soft things as other men have said,
that you'll remember. For you need not so.
Give them not praise. For, deaf, how should they know
it is not curses heaped on each gashed head?
Nor tears. Their blind eyes see not your tears flow.
Nor honour. It is easy to be dead.
Say only this, 'They are dead.' Then add thereto,
'Yet many a better one has died before.'
Then, scanning all the o'ercrowded mass, should you
perceive one face that you loved heretofore,
it is a spook. None wears the face you knew.
Great death has made all his for evermore.

5th BN — North Staffordshire Regiment — **6th BN**

13th October 1915
STOKE-ON-TRENT'S
BLACKEST DAY
"LEST WE FORGET"

HOHENZOLLERN REDOUBT

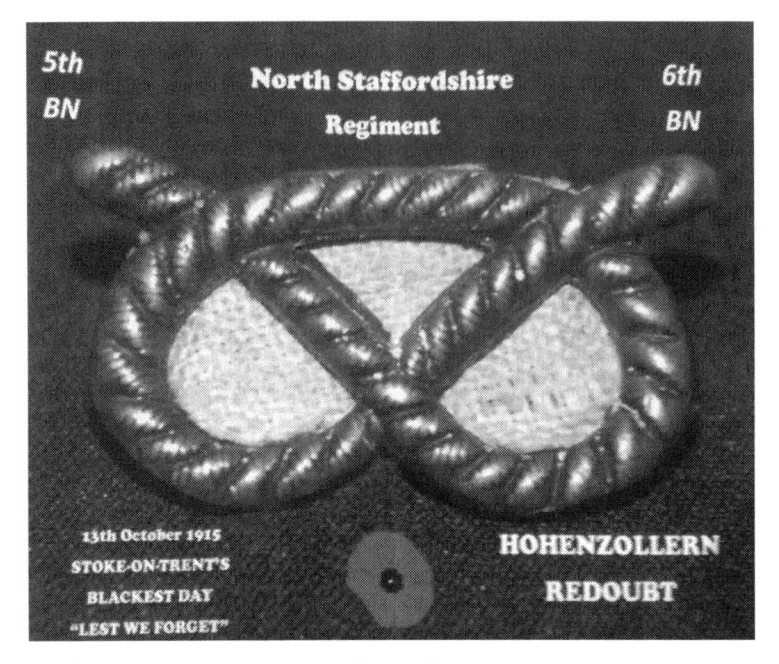

The photograph dedicated to the Hohenzollern Redoubt made by Mr Phil Rowley.

In the creation of this book, I thought it right to publicly thank the people of Staffordshire and beyond who helped me, so I complied the following letter.

"To all the people who helped me with my project to create my book, from all over Stoke and Staffordshire, and beyond, I am very grateful for the wealth of information you have given me, it has been very helpful. The book title will be "Hell at Hohenzollern, October 13th 1915, Staffordshire's Blackest Day"

My proposal was viewed by two publishers, who turned me down, but there is another publisher interested. To me it means the world to tell the story of our fallen stoke men who went over the top shouting potters for ever!
My life too has been a battle, from birth I've had surgery,

heart surgery as a baby, and then when I was 19 I had lung and emergency stomach surgery. Many people ask me if you enjoy learning about the military so much why don't you join, well I can't because I'm medically unfit for active service, so my way of taking part is studying them. I am hoping I can make something from this, my dad has suggested using the money my grandparents left me as it what they would have wanted to fund the publication, to which I thought yes they would.

So there is my story, if anyone has any information on the attack on the Hohenzollern Redoubt, or who is related to a soldier who fell on October 13th 1915 and who hasn't contacted me before, or if you have would just like a chat about my book and ideas, please email me on...."[62]

On January 26th 2015 a Mr David Smith aged 59 of Porthill contacted me via text message, after some confusion about what he meant in his text I worked out what he meant and from this I have created this brief story on his Grandfather.

Private Henry (h

Harry) Smith. 1869-1965.

Private Henry was born in 1896. Aged 18, in 1914 he lived in Hall Street, Tunstall. He had two older brothers, Tom and Charles. Charles lost his life at Kut in 1916 whilst in action in Mesopotamia, modern day Iraq. He enlisted into the 1/5th North Staffordshire Regiment on January 23rd 1914 and his Regiment number was 200208. During the attack on the Hohenzollern Henry was shot in the shoulder. After treatment he was sent home for some leave and to recuperate. What David told me next interested me greatly. The parents of Captain Reginald Tavenor Johnson arrived in what Henry believes was a posh looking Rolls Royce car. They wanted to ask the young man how their son had

---

[62] The sentinel, January 24th 2015, The way we were issue 176 pp:11.

died as Henry was in his company during the attack, and on leaving Johnson's father gave Henry £5 for his information on their son's fate.

David told me how he remembers his Grandfather as he died when he was 10 years old. He told me that Henry used to teach him Morse code with a flashlight and said what a Gentleman he was and that he spent the rest of his life, working down Whitfield pit. Along with his First World War medals he also received the Home guard medal for service during the Second World War. They in time will be inherited by his grandson who is now two years old. In addition to this David told me that his Great Grandfather Arthur Adams served in the Boer War aged just 14 and then during the Great war with the Royal Horse Artillery.

Another man who contacted me after seeing my second Sentinel article went by the name of Simon Wakeling and sent me the following Email.

Hi Callan,

I read your article in the evening sentinel 24.01.15 in which you ask for any relatives of those lost at Hohenzollern to get in touch and thought it best to contact you as my great uncle was killed in that action.

I come from a long standing family from Stone staffs, and my Nan went into St Marys care home for her last years and she always looked out of the window at an old door step across the road that was now part of the pavement. It was on that doorstep that she waved goodbye to her big brother - who she never saw again. His name was George and she asked me to find where he was buried, as they were never told back in the war.

I promised to do so and here is what I found....

My Great Uncles name was George Rowson private 2247 1st 5th Battalion North Staffs Regiment who was killed in action on 13th October 1915.

No doubt you have reviewed the war diary covering this action at the Staffs Regimental museum. In Aug 1999 I drafted a short research paper on my Great Uncle and shared this with my family. By way of background my family roots are in Stone and George is included on the war memorial in the town centre.

It was also a great honour last year when my wife nominated Georges name for the national poppy memorial at the tower of London, where the names of randomly chosen soldiers were read out by the Lord Lieutenant during the last post. Details can be found in the IWM archive which shows the recording on DVD of these nightly memorials for the nation.

I managed to review the war diaries and then transposed the maps onto a recent French map, and during a visit to France in 1999 we were able to locate the battlefield, cemetery in the quarry and little chapel that still remains on the battlefield, so were confident that we had identified the trenches ' big Willie', 'Hulluch Alley' and 'Central Boyau' where the battle was fought. We videotaped the visit in which I kick an unexploded 12 inch shell on the side of the path!

George was interned at the cemetery at Bulley Greney, pas de Calais, France grave ref no VII.B.3. We have visited Georges grave on many occasions and in the hope that we can locate his best friends Lou Plimmer's grave, although sadly it looks like Lou's grave is unmarked....so perhaps the grave next to Georges is that of his best friend who he left Stone with him to enlist and who died at his side that day in Hohenzollern. If you have information on Lou Plimmer we would love to hear it?

I'm not sure if you have visited the battlefield , but it is a real shock as I had imagined that the Hohenzollern was a hill when in fact the enemy machine guns were probably only 3 ft higher - enough that day to get a clean line of fire onto our lads. Very sad.

Anyway I hope this information is useful and it would be good to hear where you have got to with your book and publishing deal, as it would be a great memorial to the lads we lost that sad day. Simon Wakeling

There was one man who contacted me who gave more than I could possibly have ever imagined reciving, his name was Mr David Malkin, and the next chapter will focus on his Relative, Sergeant Major Ernest Godfrey Thomas.

Chapter four: The short life Ernest Godfrey Thomas. 1890-1915.

Of all the men who died on October 13th 1915, why has this man been picked for his own chapter? The simple reason is this is a unique account of one man's short life, and that of his best friend who also died on the same day. This information was kindly sent to me via email, from Mr David Malkin, a resident of Witney in Oxfordshire. Mr Malkin introduced himself to me with the following email.

14th October 2014.

Hi Mr Chevin. I was very interested indeed to read your article about the 5th North. My Mothers brother Sgt Major Ernest Godfrey Thomas was killed on 13th October 1915.My family have recently found a series of letters from Ernest just before he joined up and from the front line. I have been through then all and have printed the most interesting accounts of life at the front. His best friend was Phil York of Stone who was killed on the same day. Would you like me to e mail them to you? I also have some photographs. Let me know... I am David Malkin. I was born in the potteries in 1928 and our family made tiles in Burslem. My father Roy Malkin married Lilian Thomas in 1923. Her cousin was Billie Robinson son of WE Robinson Mayor of Stoke on Trent during WW1. After 20 years in the USA I now live near my daughter in Witney Oxford. I look forward to hearing from you. There is a book called The History of the 5th North Staffords which has a photo of my father and Billie Robinson. I lent my copy to someone and they lost it! Best wishes.

David Malkin

Obviously amazed and interested I had to learn more , the email carried on describing his connection to Hohenzollern and that he had letters from his relative, and I immediately asked if I could see them.

Mr Malkin was kind enough to send me the following information to use in the book.

Before we look at this fascinating story lets' learn a little bit about David Malkin. I sent an email to this generous man asking if he had any memories of living in the potteries. Mr Malkin replied

"One of my early memories was seeing the R 101 on a proving flight over Stoke on Trent, before it crashed on its way to India."

Mr Malkin was born at The Limes 1st Avenue Porthill in 1928. He wrote to me, "A memory I have of Nov 11th in the early 30's was driving with my, mother up Porthill. At exactly 11.am all the traffic stopped for two minutes. I think that was when I first heard about my mother's brother Ernest. Another memory is of the yellow smog, when it was foggy and there were several hundred bottle ovens belching smoke into the atmosphere" He was sent to school from 1937 to 1946. In 1946 he then joined the army for two years, and then the TA for six years. Mr Malkin took the honours course in ceramics from 1948 to 1950 and joined the family company. Malkin Tiles. His Father died in 1951 and His Grandfather Sydney in 1953. He told me that his father did not serve in France during the Great War. He was posted to Ely in Cambridgeshire with a searchlight unit, to watch for Zeppelins coming in over the East Coast. The best position for this was on the Tower of Ely Cathedral.

Mr Malkin spent his whole life in the Ceramic Industry, first with Malkin Tiles and later with H & R Johnsons Richards Tiles, after the great mergers of 1968. In 1971 he became a founder trustee of the Gladstone Pottery Museum and for eighteen years was chairman of the Stoke on Trent Festival. In January 1991 he went to the USA on behalf of Johnsons to develop sales of tile for floor tile restoration purposes. He retired from Johnsons in 1997 and with his son James formed his own company to continue in Floor tile restoration. He retired in 2009 and returned to UK

Mr Malkin revealed to me in a telephone conversation that these letters were a recent discovery, in fact within the last year. They had been filed away for the past 40 years and were discovered just in time for the Great War centenary. Luckily Mr Malkin, with the agreement of his family decided to share them with me for the purpose of this book.

David Malkin's introduction to Ernest's letters.

From the large number of letters of condolence and personal letters from Ernest to his family, I have tried to piece together the short life of Uncle Ernest, my mother and Aunt Mabel's brother. I am David Malkin. Ernest's nephew.

His Grandparents were Uriah Thomas and Martha Lowndes. Married circa 1856

Ernest's Parents were George and Mary Rose Thomas. They married in 1888. She was the daughter of William Robinson and Jane Robinson nee Corn. The Brother of Mary Rose, (Nickname Pollie) was W E Robinson Mayor of Stoke throughout World War 1 and later MP for Burslem.

Ernest's best friend was Phil York Irvin who lived at Granville, Stone.

I do not know where Ernest went to school, but in the 1911 census said he lived at home, Melbourne, Albert Terrace, Wolstanton, with his family. He is described as an Electrical Engineer. I now know he trained with the Electricity Works in Burslem before going to work for John Brown Ltd of Sheffield. The following are extracts from letters both before and during W W 1.

There are two undated letters from Ernest which are obviously pre First World War, and are posted in Sheffield. The actual letters are in italics.

Ernest Godfrey Thomas. Aged 25.

Dear Mother. "Thanks very much for the suit, kerchiefs shirt and socks, they are all the correct size. Will you ask Mr Venables if he will send me "That Song of Sleep. I shall be removing this weekend, and have made arrangements for Lily to spend three or four days with me at Whales. You might let me know what holidays she has and when it will be most suitable for her to come. I shall get two days holiday at Whit, but not together otherwise I should come home. How is father getting along at the works, and Mabel? You never say anything about them in your letters.. I am going to Weston Park on Monday, Firth Park on Tuesday which is quite close to us, to hear the bands which are playing in the various parks every day of the week. I enclose programme for this week. I should be pleased to receive two pairs of drawers, like the one you got me. I have been looking out for some time but they are all long ones. I should like them before I go to the Whales. I was introduced to one of the Head Officials of the corporation, by the Whales. He gets £1000 per year. Not a bad post is it! These are the men who might be of some use to me. You never say anything about Auntie Carrie. Just tell her I shall be pleased to receive that cake. How did the sermons go off? What did they get? What about my dress suit? I am going to see "Hello Tango" tonight so must close now as it is nearly tea time. Hoping you are all keeping well. Yours Ernest.

86 Bellhouse Rd, Shergreen, Firth Park, Sheffield.

"I am going to try and come home on Tuesday in time for the meeting at the Drill Hall. I shall join the Battalion. I am in very good health. I hope all are at home. No news from here. I shall go to the Lowndes on Monday. John Browns will be only too pleased to keep my place open. A married man will take it for the present. If you haven't returned my uniform get father to ring the drill hall up at Shelton. Speak to Sgt Major Dewsnap and tell him that I am returning home to join the Coy again, and can I keep my uniform. Ask him to do this for me on Monday. If Dewsnap is not there, speak to the officer in charge. Now goodbye for the present. Working hard. Love to all Ernest.

Ernest seems to have re-joined the TA. Presumably he had to leave it when he went to Sheffield.

The local TA Regiment was the 1st 5th Battalion North Staffordshire Regiment which many local people joined including my father Roy, and Ernest's cousin Bill Robinson " Billie". The unit was formed in August 1914 as part of The Staffordshire Brigade, North Midland Division. They initially trained at Butterton and then in November 1914, went to Bishops Stortford. They landed in France at Le Havre in March 1915, and on 12th May became 137th Brigade. North Midlands Division. The 1st 5th Battalion was one of the first TA Units to go to France and in 1915 were involved in the Battle of Loos and the Hohenzollern Redoubt. In 1916 they were sent to Egypt

The following are extracts from letters sent home before Ernest went to France. These are from Bishops Stortford, Luton and Saffron Waldon. The dates are difficult to determine as very few are shown.

Dear Mother,

"The box arrived safely on Sunday morning, with the contents intact, for which I thank you very much. I have been promoted to Lance Corporal which brings me 3 pence per day more. So please address letters to that effect. I have no cleaning to do now. I do not know when we are going away, but Capt Wood said early this week, but I attach little importance to it as I have heard so many of these fairy tales. But anyway I have heard that I had to be inoculated on Monday. If you could advance me my train fare I might get home this next week end. You see we have to pay for our tickets on Wednesday and we get paid on Friday. It is a bit rotten but you could have it back when I get home. I have been issued with a new suit of uniform. 1 shirt, 2 prs Boots 1 pr pants and undervest. 1 Cardigan Jacket and 1 pr of slippers, 1 body belt, so I will send some of my own home. Write by return and let me know what you can do. I should require 10 shillings. Love to all Ernest."

PS. Thank Auntie Maud for the oatcakes. I have written to Auntie Annie, and thank Mrs Shaw. I went to see Reg this morning. He is a long way from me, but looks very well- much better situated than I!

Saffron Walden

Dearest All, Many thanks for your letter. Will you please get me another elastic anklet from Cornwells size 7. I have had a letter and 50 cigs from The Laurels. Is it George Wellington who they are from, or Cissie? I just don't know!.. I cannot tell if you are to expect me home for Xmas yet.   (This must be 1914.) I have been promoted to Full Corporal. I will write you this week end. This is a dead end place. One Picture Palace. I am quite well. Yours Ernest.

Dear Father, Thanks so much for your PO. I cannot tell you what time I shall get home, in fact I have not yet received my pass. I have just recovered from my inoculation which gave me a lot of trouble. We are still working very hard, but I have no idea when we are going away. The nearest possible time I can tell you will be 2am Saturday morning at Stoke. So if Uncle Willie is kind enough to send his car for me, I should be greatly obliged. Otherwise I shall have to walk. See what you can do. Perhaps Billie can come to meet me. Ernest.
Bishops Stortford.

"Dearest Mother, The parcel you sent me arrived quite safely. I have managed to find some of my things from Luton and I have had them forwarded on to me. So now I shall be able to send some home. I shall simply carry one complete change. We have about the same amount of work to do but the food is much better. The government pay 9 pence per day for each man and some people have as many as 10 men billeted on them. Of course they have to do the cooking, and we find the rations. There is an outbreak of measles here, but it is not amongst the troops. The streets where this outbreak occurred is now out of bounds. I still have a bed to sleep in though others are less fortunate. I had to go round all the billets last Friday to settle up for the 10 days we have been here. I have little time to myself now.. The colour Sergeant has been temporary promoted to Sergt Major, so his place is being taken by a Sergt and myself. The Sergt is responsible for the discipline of the company and I for the reports wages and billets for which I am going to get 6 pence per day extra. This will make my wages 2 Shillings. (Per day) Now I am expecting to get another stripe. I am going to get all I can. I never get to bed now before 11.0pm, but I don't attend all parades. I had a busy day on Sunday making 122 insurance cards out and stamping them for our company. Today we should go for a Divisional Route March carrying our full equipment which we always do. The distance is 13 ½ miles and the total weight of our equipment is 90lbs. We hear nothing about moving. In fact we hear very little about the war. I have posted the letter to Browns. How is Billie getting on at Butterton? We have all been issued with new rifles so I expect our old ones are going to Butterton. The ones we have now have a much stronger barrel and fire a higher velocity cartridge. I have been enjoying the best of health, never even had a cold. I must close now and get some work done. Give my love to all. Hoping you are all well. Love Ernest.

Mr Malkin added I think we can assume that Billie is his cousin Bill Robinson, son of the Mayor of Stoke, his mothers' brother. Billie was commissioned into the 5th North Staffords just after my father.

Phil York Irwin aged 21.

Post card from Phil York Irwin. (Ernest's best friend) dated 2ND March 1915.

"Dear Mrs Thomas. We arrived in Southampton yesterday. Ernest has had to go on guard at the boat so has asked me to send you a card, as he cannot write himself. We are billeted in a school sleeping on the floor for a change. Please excuse the scrawl, but the conditions are adverse for writing.

Yrs Sincerely. Phil H York Irwin."

Military historian Andrew Thornton kindly supplied me with the following information of Phil York Irwin.

Philip Irwin was born at Barlaston in 1894 and was the only son of Henry and Alice Irwin, who lived at Granville in Stone. Henry Irwin was a Justice of the peace. Philip had been educated at Tanllwyfan School at Old Colwyn and later at the forest school in Walthamsow, where he was made a member of the cadet's corps He enjoyed playing sport and was a member of the Cricket, Golf and Tennis clubs in Stone. Irwin enlisted in the 5th North Staffords at Hanley on the 7th of September 1914 and went to France with No.1 platoon, a company of the $1/5^{th}$ Battalion. He qualified as a bomber and was appointed Lance-Sergeant. In October 1915 Lieutenant-Colonel Knight had selected him to be sent home to be commissioned as a Second-Lieutenant in the $3/5^{th}$ Battalion, however this did not happen as Lance Sergeant Irwin went into action with the $1/5^{th}$ North Staffords on October 13th 1915 at the Hohenzollern Redoubt. He was a member of one of the Battalion's bombing parties and was mortally wounded during the fighting to take the German trenches around the redoubt. He died of his injuries the day after the attack on October 14th 1915. His body was not identified after the war and his name was carved on the Loos Memorial. Philip Irwin is also remembered on the war memorial in stone.

British Expeditionary Force. France.

"Dearest Mother. At last we are in France. We had a pleasant crossing from Southampton to Havre and from the latter place we entrained for a destination unknown, but anyway it took us 24 hours to get there. We are now within hearing distance of the firing. We are billeted in a barn and I find my little bit of French very useful. I have not had my clothes off for over a week but I hope to have a change here. Send me some tobacco & cigs as I cannot get any here. How is Billie getting along? I expect he will be joining us when the first lot of reserves come out. Send me a Sentinel. I have a sheep skin coat and look like a Teddy bear, but they are very warm. We have seen several aeroplanes so you can guess the distance we are from Jerry lines. In fact I expect we shall be there when you receive this letter. Have you received my music and parcels from Saffron Walden yet? Remember me to all at home and tell them I am in the best of health. I would like to write, but I have very little time now. Tell them to write to me. Thank Auntie Carrie for her letter. I am pleased to hear she is better. I had a letter from Auntie Annie Buckley just before I left. We have been having biscuits and corned beef for the last two days.. Love to all Ernest.

France 16th April 1915

Dearest Mother. Thanks so much for the parcel. I got it the same day as we returned to the rest camp after being in the trenches 5 days. Here we have a band performing every afternoon which is very enjoyable. When are you going to send me some disinfectant? Hurry up. Will you get me a nice tea service and send it to Miss E Newey, East Lodge, Dunwood Road, Bishops Stortford Hertford as she is getting married at the end of this month. Irwin and I were billeted there and they were so kind to us. So I feel I would like to send her something. Tell Auntie Maud I shall write to her and thank her for her kindness. We have many tunes in the trenches from the mouth organ she sent. Also thank Frank for the cigs. I have written to Mr Crossley, so he will probably come to see you. I am in the best of health. Now Goodbye. Love to all Ernest.

Belgium 24th April 1915.

"Dearest Father and Mother. Just a few lines to let you know I am still in the best of health. I had the pleasure of being spoken to by Sir John French while standing outside our rest camp. He inquired if the men were in good health and being fed well. What have you done about that tea service? Let me know as soon as possible. Try and send me a Daily Sentinel as well as the Weekly. I could do with a wrist watch. I will write to Mrs Dunning, but in the meantime thank her for the lighter. It is most useful in the trenches. Love to all. Hoping you are all in the best of health. Ernest."

Belgium. 1st May 1915.

"Dearest Mother and Father, Again I have returned to the rest camp. We had a grand time in the trenches. The weather was glorious. Will you send me a change of linen for the 11th as I expect to be in the rest camp again by that date? I received your parcel safely. It came before your letter. The soups are A1. Please don't send me any more tobacco. We get plenty of it out here, and if we run short we can get plenty of tobacco leaf which has been left at the farms. Only send me some decent cigs occasionally- one every two weeks. Nothing very exciting has happened here this week. The Germans made an air attack near Ypres and the French retired but the Canadians came up and held the position. Irwin has returned from Hospital and is quite well again. We share our parcels. I have not heard from Mr Crossley yet. Mr Edwards has sent me a fine penknife and some papers. I have also had a tin of cigs from Mrs Whale and some photos of the Bungalow at Rudyard.. What was Tom Jones like? Must close now. Yours Ernest."

Belgium 7th May 1915.

"Dearest Mother and Father. We are simply having glorious weather out here. I am now going through a course of bomb throwing along with Irwin, which we find very interesting. I received the parcel you sent which was quite useful. The watch you mention in your letter will also be quite useful. Be sure to see that it is in proper working order before you send it.. Now I am short of a clasp knife with a tin opener complete, towel shaving brush and kerchiefs, bachelor buttons, pair of braces. See if you can get a chain to fasten the knife on, also see if you can get a good respirator for me to use against those asphyxiating gases. Send these articles as soon as possible. I am in the best of health and quite brown. In fact it is doing me good. I never have enjoyed better health. Love to all and thanks for the parcel. Ernest."

3rd June 1915.

"Dearest Father and Mother, Just returned to rest camp. We are having glorious weather and the country around looks absolutely fine. On the way to our trenches we walked under an avenue of trees for about three miles, at both ends of which are two ruined villages. The one nearest the trenches is absolutely raised to the ground. I have just received your parcel. I am so glad you have sent me some tablets to purify the water as it is getting very bad. All the water we have to drink has to be boiled. The fruit is most refreshing during this hot weather. I gave an exhibition of how to fi9re rifle grenades to our colonel, also to the officers and NCO's while in the trenches this time. I am also sending home a German rifle grenade which the Germans sent over to our trenches, and which didn't explode so I took it to pieces. It is the best souvenir it is possible to get, so take care of it.. What does Uncle Willie think of my collection? I had a fine box of cigs from John Brown. Isn't it good of them? I also had a letter from Billie on 2nd June. He seems to be getting on well. The watch Father sent me continues to keep splendid time. In the next parcel send me a drinking mug- not too large. Remember me to all my friends. I am keeping in the best of health. Love to all Ernest"2

Belgium 1st September 1915.

"Dearest Mother and Father. I am now in my new quarters so am very comfortable. My address is now Sgt Major! No 2951, Headquarters 137th Infantry Brigade 46th Division, so let all my friends at home know it is my new address. I have just received a parcel from Auntie Carrie, so please thank her for it. Say I am writing to her this week. I am in the very best of health. Love to all Ernest."

Mr Malkin wrote

This next letter is dated 27th September, from Belgium, but it is difficult to tell to whom it was sent. It is very interesting so I am including it in this collection. It starts

2nd Lt Billie Robinson. 5th North Staffords. Cousin of Ernest Godfrey Thomas.

Son of Uncle Willie Robinson Mayor of Stoke on Trent 1914 – 1918.

Brother of Mary Rose (Pollie) Thomas.

Ernest's Cousin Billie,

"Dearest Jnr. (I am sure he is writing to his cousin Billie Robinson)I am so sorry I have been such a long time answering your last interesting letter, but you must excuse me this time owing to the fact that we have been so busy. We have again moved and taken over some more trenches so this is the hottest place I have been in yet. We have such a lot of shell fire which is always a great strain. I have had one very narrow escape, a small high explosive burst a yard from me it simply smothered me in soil. On 25th September one of our aeroplanes was set fire to a Bosh by machine gun fire, just over our lines. It was a fine sight. The Bosh observer fell out when he was about 6000ft in the air, but the driver brought the aeroplane down safely, but he was burnt to death. We sent up such a cheer when the Bosh was on fire. The first days in the trenches this time have been the worst I have experienced. We have had plenty of rain and I have been wet through. In some places the water was 1 foot deep. During the time we were in the trenches 5 mines have been exploded, but they have not blown us up, although the Leicester's have suffered fairly heavily. When we are making new trenches we have to take great care as men are buried all over the place. A great fight took place here. In some of the graves as many as 60 are buried. Our trenches in places are as near as 5 yards from the Bosh, so we have to keep a very strict lookout. Now I must close. Hoping you will write soon. Love to all. Ernest."

The following is probably the last letter written by Ernest before he was killed in action on 13th October 1915.

Somewhere on the Western Front October 1915.

"Dearest Mother and Father. I am sorry not to have written before and I hope you will excuse me. I am now attached to the Brigade Staff and I have been made Temp Act Sgt Major, and QM Sgt to the Brigade Grenadier Company. I have a fine billet, one just to have my meals in, and the other to sleep in. The majority of my work is out of the trenches, although occasionally I have to go in just for a day or so. The late Sgt Major was wounded, so he was evacuated. I have not yet received my weekly parcel although the last has given me the news and latest messages from you.. My chief work is instructing Bomb Throwers, and looking after the supply of bombs. I have a splendid officer and we get along well together. Colonel Knight wanted me to stay with the Battalion (5th North), but I told him I wanted promotion, so he said he was sorry to lose me, and said I had done very well. I cannot say when I shall get leave now, but I stand a much better chance now. I am hoping to see Percy Wain tomorrow. Now goodbye, and love to all. Ernest."

This is the announcement from the Staffordshire Sentinel.

> **KILLED.**
>
> **SERGT. MAJOR ERNEST G. THOMAS.**
>
> News has been received by Mr. and Mrs. Geo. W. Thomas, of Albert-terrace, Wolstanton, that their son, Sergt. Major Ernest G. Thomas, of the 1st-5th North Staffords, was killed in action in the attack on the 13th inst.
>
> Sergt.-Major Thomas was formerly employed at the Electricity Works, Burslem, and afterwards with Messrs. John Brown and Co., Sheffield. He obtained leave of absence and returned to enlist as a private in the 2nd-5th North Staffords on the formation of that battalion in September, 1914. He was in training with them for a short period at Butterton, and left for Flanders with the 1st-5th as a corporal. He was recently promoted to staff sergeant-major, and was acting as instructor in bomb-throwing. He was one of five recently selected for promotion to commissioned rank. His death is deeply regretted by a wide circle of friends, and much sympathy is felt for his parents and sisters in their bereavement.

[63]

The article from the sentinel announcing Ernest's death, date October 30th 1915.

The last letter in this collection is from his cousin 2nd Lt Billie Robinson. 5th Battalion N S Regt, dated 25th November 1915, addressed to his Aunt, Mary Rose Thomas. My Grandmother.

"My dear Auntie, I have at last reached the trenches after having been meandering about the line for several days looking for the 5th North. I am posted to A Coy under Captain Worthington and am getting on in fine style. I have been making a lot of enquiries about Ernest and everyone I

---

[63] The Staffordshire evening sentinel October 30th 1915 pp:8

asked had always got a good word for him. They said that he led the attack as Captain Johnson had been killed as soon as he was over the parapet, and was the first to reach the first line of German trenches. He was wounded twice before he got there but still continued to throw his bombs until he fell. He was buried in the German trench which is now held by the Guards, six hundred yards in front of the English trenches. I do not know where, but as time goes on we may be moved there again and then I will look around. He was one of the most popular men in the Battalion. Last night was my first night in the trenches. I shall always remember it as they shelled us for over an hour with their heavy guns. When they had finished our R F A started and put 800 shells onto a new trench they had been building and absolutely washed it out. I thought I should have had an attack of the nerves, but as a matter of fact it was just the opposite, like drinking champagne. Nobody seems to take much notice of the guns going off than of a carriage passing in the street. Everybody is so jolly playing cards and other games when the bombardment is on. I have never seen anything like it. We go out of the trenches tonight for three days at the rest camp so I shall be able to post this when I go up. Love to all Billie.

What made this generous offer to use these extracts was the fact Mr Malkin included extracts from some of the very many letters of condolence received by the Thomas family following the announcement of Ernest's death.

There are three letters from Mrs Irwin of Stone, Mother of Ernest's best friend Phil Irwin, who must have been killed about the same time as Ernest.

Granville, Stone Staffs. October 23rd 1915.

"Dear Mrs Thomas. I feel I must write you a few words because both our hearts are well nigh broken with this crushing sorrow. Our two dear brave high spirited boys, gone from us when we thought all was well with them and that they were coming home to enjoy their well-earned honours. It is cruel and bitter, but God is helping us to bear it and I pray that you and yours may be helped to have each other's prayers, I know. I was thinking of you with deep anxiety when I feared your dear boy had gone, before I knew that my grief was yours. The sorrow for them and the pride in them is intense. With heartfelt sympathy, yours sorrowfully, Alice M Irwin."

November 13th 1915

"My dear Mrs Thomas, We shall think of you all tomorrow during the service for your dear boy. I hope you are feeling better, 'tho I am afraid it will be a long time before you can think calmly of this sorrow. It is so crushing and seems to overwhelm and crowd everything else out of life. Perhaps this is wrong and we have to fight against it. We mothers alone know the heart breaking sense of loss. We have loved them as intensely since the hour of their birth and so many hopes fears and wishes have been mapped up in them, that part of oneself seems gone, but we can love them still and think of them in the fuller life to where they have gone, and rejoice that they have proved themselves true men and heroes. Our love and pride will never die and God will comfort us and in time his healing balm and peace will fill our hearts. In the meantime we must have courage, and take up our cross daily and remember a prayer for the thousands of mothers who are weeping for their sons. Well we have both been blessed with a dear good boy and we thank God for him. With all loving thoughts, I am dear Mrs Thomas, Yrs Sincerely Alice M Irwin.

The Last letter from Mrs Irwin dated was Dec 7th 1915.

"My dear Mrs Thomas. Mrs Robinson, (wife of the Mayor of Stoke on Trent) kindly asked me over tomorrow to meet you and much as I would have liked to do so, I cannot manage it. I'm not feeling too well just now. This change in the weather has upset me. I felt much brighter during the frost and the days are so short and dark now, and we have no man to drive the car, that I must defer the pleasure of seeing you. I've been going to write to ask you over to see me. It would be nice if you could come to lunch and we could have a nice quiet talk. Would any day next week suit you, or would you rather leave it until after Xmas? We are expecting Major Bache over one day and it will probably be tomorrow, 'tho he could not say exactly.. I expect that you have by now heard a few more details about your darling boy. I heard splendid things about him the other day. How grandly and fearlessly he behaved in the charge, a perfect hero. A young fellow home on leave in Stone came to see me and he was told this about Ernest. They couldn't stop him. Again and again he went back for bombs. Oh, these dear fearless boys. How cruel it seems!. I've heard a lot about Phil too, but not anything about the 13th. I saw one of the bombers yesterday, but he was relegated to the 6th South for that charge and only heard the news of our boys the day after. He was told how great Ernest was.. With love, and earnestly hoping you are feeling better, Yrs Sincerely Alice M Irwin."

Mr Malkin's own research confirmed that Phil Irwin was a Lance Sergeant in the 5th North Staffords and was killed on the same day as Ernest.

Going back in time we see a letter from Annie (Pollie's sister) of 56 Wickham Way, Parklangley, Beckenham, and Dated 26th Oct 1915.

"My very dear Pollie, (Nickname of Mary Rose Thomas?) Words can't express my love and feelings for you at this sad time. We are very grieved, and you know dear you have our deepest sympathy. This is a very very sad time for parents, especially Mothers, but you have the consolation that your boy died a noble and glorious death. The grandest death of all fighting for his country, and dearest, you must try to think of it in that light and try not to fret too much for your own sake and for the sake of those around you. You must both feel proud to be the parents of such a good brave and clever soldier. I wrote to Ernest at the time you asked me to do so, but have had no answer, so I'm afraid he

Never got my letter. Sam Buckley's son is at the front. He is with the Canadians and has been there for months. Lizzie's second boy expects to go any time and she the poor thing is very sad. How are Will's boys? Are they still spared, I hope so. If I was near to you we could meet oftener. We had a terrible fright a fortnight ago, when a Zeppelin passed over here. The noise was terrific, from the guns and we could see the shells bursting and the bombs dropping, from Violets bedroom. It lit up her room and shook the bed. They fell on Croydon about 3 to 5 miles away. We felt our lives were not worth much. This is the second time they have been over here. But we must think of what our boys are doing for us, it seems small. Please write when you feel able and thank George for sending the paper. With very fond love to you all, Your Loving Annie."

This is from Mary Rose's (Pollies) sister Annie Radford.

47 Greetwell Gate, Lincoln 25/10/ 15.

"My Dear Lilly and Mabel, (Sisters of Ernest) I feel I must write to try to express how very sorry I am to hear of your overwhelming sorrow.. There are so many sad hearts at this time. I shall be thankful when this terrible war is ended. Ernest was such a fine fellow, always so bright and jolly with everybody. He died doing his duty, and has gone to his reward. Yours with love and sympathy. Connie. Elliot ? Chatfield.?"

Northern Ley, Alsager Cheshire.6/11/15.

"Dear Pollie, I was so grieved to see in the Sentinel that your dear boy Ernest had been killed in action---- James and I felt we should write you a line and trust that God who knows all our sorrows will help you to be brave through all this trouble, to feel that your darling boy died such a noble death to save his country. With Love. Lizzie Dudson. Cousin. Daughter of Annie Burgess nee Corn."

The Laurels, St George's Wellington Salop. 9 Nov 15.

"Dear Pollie and George. Both Frank and I wish to send you our deepest sympathy. ---He was a good and brave lad and I know would give his life ungrudgingly for his country. Yours affectionately, Cissie Upton Nee Sant. (Cousin) Daughter of Mary Corn."

Cissie was the mother of Kathleen Cooper, whose husband was killed in 1914.

63 Norwood Rd, Sheffield.24/11/15.

"Dear Mrs Thomas, Will you accept from all of us our best love and sympathy in the loss of your son. Somehow we never thought he would give his life for his country and we were looking forward to the time when this dreadful war would be over and we should spend more happy times together as we used to before he left Sheffield. He gave us one of his songs and left a music book, and if you would like to have them we will send them on, 'tho we should like to keep the song. Yrs very sincerely, Nellie Boothby."

206 Abbeyfield Road, Pitsmoor, Sheffield. Oct 22/1915.

"My dear Mrs Thomas. What can I say to you? No words of mine can be any possible comfort to you, but believe me my heart and thoughts are with you and yours continually during this time of terrible suspense I hope it may help and comfort you that he was bravely fighting to defend us, his king and his country from those awful Germans and their murderous methods. Dear old Ernest, he grew very deeply into my affections the first time I met him and I have always taken a great interest in him and his doings. I earnestly trust the time will come when I shall see him and take him by the hand again. Please give my love to lil. Yours affectionately, Hannah Whale." Tommy's Mother?

206 Abbeyfield Rd, Pitsmoor, Sheffield. 26 Oct 15.

"My dearest Mrs Thomas, It is impossible for me to convey in this letter the deep sympathy we have for you all in the great trouble that has fallen upon you. ----Remember dear Mrs Thomas that though death seems to be the end it is really only the gateway through which Ernest has passed to that brighter country where there is no more pain or sorrow and where in the future we shall all meet again—Mother is writing to you soon, but at present she is ill in bed. We were all so fond of Ernest and I am sure Mother seemed to look upon him as her own boy. With my fondest love and every kind thought, I remain your loving other daughter, Tommy." (Possibly Ernest's girlfriend. She was also a good friend of my mother Lilian and I remember meeting her)

211 Waterloo Road, Burslem 23rd Oct 15.

"My dear dear Mrs Thomas. It is hard to believe that the loving little boy when he was two years old, and taken for a walk most days of the week along Rushton Road, by Auntie Carrie and Auntie Maud, would give up his tall splendid manhood, his life for mothers and sisters and little ones. At times I expect it would be worse than death if it were not for those grand boys who are giving themselves. They can give no more. ----- In deep grief, yours sincerely Elizabeth G Baines."

Mr Malkin believes this was the daughter of Harry Burgess and Anne Corn, who married the father of Charley and Lily Baines etc.

Ravenscliffe, Porthill. 20/10/15

"Dear Mr and Mrs Thomas. Please accept our true sympathy with you in the loss of your dear brave boy. He has died a most noble death, but I quite know how you feel and trust god will be very near and comfort you. We do need his help so much in these terrible times------. Believe me in deep sorrow, yours sincerely. Mary Bennett."

Her son Harry was killed in action near Ypres on August 3rd 1915. Probably of the Dunn Bennett family.

Knowsley, 256 Waterloo Rd, Burslem. Oct 25th 1915.

"Dear Mr & Mrs Thomas, I was very grieved to hear about Ernest being killed in Belgium. I had known him practically all my life and looked upon him as one of my oldest friends, and I little thought it would be the last time I should see him when I saw him off from Stoke after his last leave. Please accept my deepest sympathy in your great loss.. Yours Sincerely Wilfred Dain."

8 Beaufort Road, Sheffield. Oct 25th.

"My dear Lil, I cannot tell you how awfully grieved we are to hear about Ernest. I want to say dear, how very sorry I am for you all in your great trouble. We grew fond of Ernest in the short time that he was in Sheffield. He was always so kind and very thoughtful for you all at home. I am sure that through your great sorrow you must be proud of one who gave his life so willingly for his country when he felt it was his duty to go. Everyone will honour his memory and honour you too for so bravely letting him go. I am afraid I can express only poorly all I would like to say to you, but I am sure you will understand me. The world seems all wrong at present and we can only hope that things get better this next year. Please give my dearest love to Mrs Thomas and your sister, and know that we feel for you all in your troubles. With Much love, yours very sincerely, Marjorie Lowndes." Mr Malkin wondered if she is related to Uriah Thomas' wife, Martha Lowndes.

Grange Cottage, Burslem Staffs. Oct 24th 1915.

"Dear Mr and Mrs Thomas, I feel I must write to tell you how truly sorry my wife and all my family are to hear of Ernest's death, and you and your family have our deepest sympathy in your very heavy bereavement.. He was always such a nice boy and we do not forget how kind he was at this time last year in calling to see Gay when he was home ill from Butterton. It is terrible that such a bright young life should be sacrificed and we can only hope that you will be given the strength to bear your loss and may God comfort you in your sorrow. Yours very sincerely F. C Jennings." This was Jennings the Tailor of Waterloo Road. This letter shows a personal connection not just to his family but it was Jennings who made one of Mr Malkin's first suits.

Ellesmere, Albert Terrace, Wolstanton.

To Mr & Mrs Thomas and Family. It is with deep regret that Mr Sherwin and I have heard of Ernest's death and we offer you our sincere sympathy in your trouble. We cannot forget that we knew him so well as a boy and what a fine man he became. Lily Sherwin.

No address. 4th Nov 1915.

"My dear Mr Thomas. It is with the deepest sorrow in my heart that I write to sympathise in the great loss you have sustained. It is poor consolation I know, but as he was one of my best friends I can do nothing less than offer you my condolences. Please accept my sincerest sympathies and believe me to be very sincerely yours, Percy N Wain."

Lightwood House, Stoke on Trent.

"My dear Lil. I feel I should like to send you just a line to tell you how truly sorry I was to hear your sad news. I can sympathise with you most sincerely having gone through almost the same trouble. However I think you can find infinite comfort from the knowledge that he has served his country. Hoping you are all as well as possible, and with heartfelt sympathy for you. With heaps of love, Lil."

Mr Malkin believes this must be Lily Baines, sister of Charley, and therefore a cousin. There was an E Baines in the 5th North Staffords who was killed early in the war

Stanley House, Rugeley 1st Nov 1915.

"Dear Mrs Thomas. I am very sorry indeed to hear of the death of your son in France. It must be a terrible blow to all of you and I beg to assure you of my sincere sympathy in your great sorrow. Yours Faithfully, John W Appleton."

Mr Malkin concluded in his documents

The above are the most interesting letters about Ernest. There are many more including official cards from the front stating that he was in good health. There was also one from the Burslem Electricity Board, and The Burslem Golf club of which he was a member.

What these documents show, is yes the story of one man, but also the strength and unity that a death of a loved one could bring to those most affected. This is a unique collection of documents that brilliantly demonstrate people's attitudes during the one of the worst times our history has ever encountered. It also shows a nationwide grief from his extended family and his former employers. There must have been thousands of letters like this about the countless men who fell not just at Loos but at all the other battles such as Gallipoli, the Somme and Ypres, but the fact Mr Malkin has discovered these and they have stood the test of time reflects their rarity and that is special, and I am sure he must be a very proud man. That is why I gave Sergeant Major Ernest Godfrey Thomas his own chapter.

Chapter Five: Remembrance in the Staffordshire area

Even as the war raged on, the people of Staffordshire were still grieving in the catastrophic losses that affected the county in 1915. Upon studying the battle it became apparent that there may be sources elsewhere, after all some of the photos of the fallen came from the newspapers in 1916, simply because their bodies had not yet been found. I checked the anniversary the year after on October 13th 1916, there was great deal on loss and memory, but the impact and losses from the Somme just a few months earlier had not yet been digested, and as a matter of fact, the Somme, was still and ongoing conflict. The year after in 1917 had a sombre piece, there had been enough time to get a rough estimate of the majority who fell on that fateful day, the third anniversary in 1918, was rather repetitive of the 1917 anniversary, so it was 1917 that the following will focus upon. What follows is a list of messages and poems in dedication to the fallen Potters, from those who loved them most, their parents, wife's and fiancées. The article was dated Saturday October 13th 1917 and was titled

BATTLE OF LOOS: SECOND ANNIVERSARY

IN MEMORIAM.

TO-DAY is the second anniversary of a fateful day in the history of the north Staffords and a dark hour in the lives of the people at home. It was in October 1915 that the first real shock of war struck the whole district and left it trembling, shaken, grief laden, but still as we have every reason to see since, undaunted and unafraid. From the date of the Battle of Loos, two years ago, anniversaries have multiplied daily, until scarcely a month, or a week, or a day that some sad soul does not keep in sacred and sorrowful remembrance. The North midland Division has been ever in the forefront of the battle and its losses from the first have been cruelly heavy. Time and time again the North Staffords have led the van of an attack.

"Where the battle's turmoil hot, there you'll find the Staffords knot"

This emotive piece is of course referring to the countless battles the North Staffords took part in up until this date. The image beneath gave the reader in 1917 a reminder of the major conflicts that the North Staffords had been involved in, this echoes the section in the introduction, which focused on the Battle of Gommecourt On July 1st 1916 and the Battle of Lens on July 1ST 1917.

Staffordshire Sentinel.

SATURDAY, OCTOBER 13th, 1917.

After Two Years.

In proud and affectionate
remembrance of the gallant
NORTH STAFFORDS
who fought and fell on
OCTOBER 13th, 1915,
also on
JULY 1st, 1916,
MARCH 13th, 1917,
JULY 1st, 1917,
and of the Staffordshire men
in various Regiments, who
sacrificed their lives on these
and other dates.

"Where are the boys of the old Brigade,
  Who fought with us side by side?
Shoulder to shoulder and blade by blade,
  Fought till they fell and died:—
Who so ready and undismayed?
  Who so merry and true?
Where are the boys of the old Brigade?
  Where are the lads we knew?"

Before we look at the messages in Memoriam, it would seem appropriate to include as this article did in the sentinel back in 1917, the opening lines of Rudyard Kipling's poem. The children. For he also shared the grief of losing his only son as did many of the people in Staffordshire, in the same battle.

"These were our children who died for our lands, they were dear in our sight.

We have only the memory left of their home treasured sayings and laughter.

The price of our loss shall be paid to our hands. Not another's hereafter

Neither the Allen nor the priest shall decide upon it. That is our right

But who shall return us the children?"[65]

The following are from the Staffordshire Sentinel, dated October 13th 1917, some are as simple as Rest easy, gone but not forgotten, or simple messages that they are missed, the ones that will be included are the most emotive and poetic from the large list.

IN MEMORIAM.

ABBOTS Frederick

He fought bravely and did his best, god grant him his eternal rest.

---

[65] The Staffordshire sentinel, Saturday October 13th 1917, pp:4

Days of sadness often come over to us, tears of sorrow often flow, but memory keeps our dear one near us, though he died two years ago.

AINSWORTH Elijah

A day of remembrance to sad to forget

ALCOCK Ernest

Forth at the buglers call, gallantly he went, midst of bayonets gleaming bright, fighting for god and right, fighting against hell and might, his life was spent.

ALLERTON Samuel

Eternal honour give, Hail! And farewell to those who died in that full spender of heroic pride that we might live.

ASHMORE Samuel

A light is from our household gone, a voice we loved is stilled, and God takes our loved ones from our homes but not from our hearts.

BARLOW, Thomas and Albert

God looked on my sons in pity, and saw them what was best, so he folded them beneath his bosom and calmly he laid them to rest, our loss in their eternal gain.

BEARD Harry

We often think of days gone by, when we were all together. A shadow on our home is east, a loved one gone forever.

BOWLER William

We think we see his smiling face, as he waved us goodbye, and left us dear ones behind to die in a foreign land, but we have one consolation, he bravely did his best, somewhere in France our dear one sleeps, a hero laid to rest, but the hardest is yet to come, when the warriors shall return and we miss among the cheering crowds the face of my dear husband.

BROUGH Lewis

He left his home in perfect health, he looked so young and brave, and he little thought how soon he would lie in a soldier's grave.

CARTLIDGE George

There is a link death cannot sever, love and remembrance lasts forever.

DOWNING Frank William

He sleeps besides his comrades, in a hallowed grave unknown, but his name is written in letters of love on the hearts he left at home.

DURBER Percy

Somewhere in France, in a lonely grave, lies my son among the brave, oh God how mysterious thy ways, to take my son in the best of his days.

FORRESTER Arthur

Two years have passed yet is still miss him, never will his memory fade, loving thoughts will always wonder, over in France where my husband is laid.

FURNIVAL William.

Gone is the one we loved so dear, silent the voice we loved to hear, too far away from sight or speech but not too far for our thoughts to reach.

GRAINGER Sydney

Friends may think that we forgot him, when at times we are apt to smile, little knowing what grief is hidden beneath the surface all the while.

HODGKINSON Joseph

These on the field of battle, he calmly took his place, he fought and died for Britain, in honour of his race.

KINSLEY Joshua

He proudly answered his countries call, and gave his life to save us all.

KNIGHT John Hall

To the memory of all the Officers, NCO'S and men of the North Staffordshire Regiment under his command.

MILLER Edward

The parting was sad, the shock severe, we little thought his end so near, tis only those who have lost can tell, the pain and grief of the one that's fell.

MITCHELL Frederick

Two years have passed, yet still I miss him, never will his memory fade, loving thoughts will always wonder over in France where our son is laid.

MORREY Henry

Sleep on dear son in a far off land, in a grave we may never see, but as long as life and memory last, we will remember thee.

RATTCLIFE.F

Honour to him in battle slain, who died that we might freedom gain.

Also from his fiancée

Death is strong but love is stronger, and though may be our bodies apart, together still in spirit and heart. I mourn the silence, unknown and unseen, and can only think of days that may have been.

SHERRATT Albert

He marched away so bravely, his young head proudly held. His footsteps never faltered. His courage never faded, then on the field of battle he calmly took his place and died in England's cause and in Honour of his Race.

SHUFFELBOTTOM.G

If we could raise his aching head, or heard his last farewell, it would not have been hard to part with one we loved so well.

SMITH Joseph

Somewhere in France their bodies be, amid the battles din, but their spirits freed deaths power deny, and leave a world of sin. Somewhere at home a tear is shed, but a trusty soul by pure faith fed just whispers, God knows best.

TUNNICLIFFE Jack

To forget him, is a vain endeavour, love and embrace lasts forever.

WARHAM George

Duty called him, he was there to do his bit, his heart was good, his spirit pure, his resting place, a soldier's grave for sure.

WASHINGTON Henry

May his reward be as great as his sacrifice

WILLIAMS

He was our only boy, so brave, nothing is left, only a grave in Flanders, named or not we do not know, do not ask us if we miss him, just give us some space.

WILLIS Colonel

Worthy our lamb that was slain, for us he was a saint, oh we miss his lovely face.

YARWOOD Henry

Dear is the grave where our boy is laid, sweet in thy memory, roses may wither, if others forget him, he will always bloom in our hearts.

Another anniversary that appeared in the Staffordshire sentinel was date October 13th 1925, the 10TH anniversary of the attack. Again a list appears with touching tributes to the fallen from the ones who knew and loved them, but as it is almost identical to the 1917 list, we shall now focus on the bulk of the 1925 article, that gives a patriotic and respectful view of how the people In the 1920s views the Great War.

STAFFORDSHIRE SENTINEL TUESDAY OCTOBER 13TH 1925

THE FIFTH NORTH STAFFORDS.

TENTH ANNIVERSARY OF THE HOHENZOLLERN.

Today is an anniversary of sad but proud memories for North Staffordshire. It is the tenth anniversary of the Hohenzollern, when the 5th North Staffordshire territorial Regiment by its courage and fearless gallantry, by its faithfulness to duty and contempt for death, by it profound patriotism proved its self-worthy of the best of England's fighting men.

THE COURSE OF THE WAR

On October 13th 1915 the war had been fourteen months in progress. The Old contemptibles had for more than a year before desperately stood in the path of the German invasion of Belgium and Northern France, covered themselves in wild glory and had laid down the foundations of ultimate victory. The Germans were so harassed by the French and British that they hastily retreated from the Marne and then began the years of intense Trench warfare. The French and British were holding up the Germans with many battles and many struggles for territory with contemporary campaigns in other areas and nearly the whole world engaged until at length, the German military octopus war laid low.

THE BATTLE OF LOOS

The 5th North Staffords went to France in March 1915, Part of the 46th midland division. In the autumn of 1915, General Joffre had discussed an offensive and asked the British to attack north of Lens. Sir John French and Sir Douglas Haig had doubts about the possibility to make an impression on the German front there, which was known to be very strong, not just in personnel but also the nature of the countryside and the nature of the industrial works, but they agreed to share in the adventure and the Battle of Loos began on September 25th 1915. The German position proving too strong for the allies, though the enemy got a good shaking.

THE HOHENZOLLERN REDOUBT

The operations on the British front eventually led to a tussle for the Hohenzollern Redoubt with varying fortunes on either side. It was ultimately decided that by the British command that one more effort should be made to capture the Hohenzollern Redoubt and it was in this effort that the 5th north Staffords freely spent themselves on October 13th 1915.

THE 5TH NORTH CASUALTIES.

That 13th October 1915 was a day that caused terrible shock to North Staffordshire. Though there had been enormous casualties in the local Regiments previously, that the 5th north Staffords had suffered, this was too many ten years ago today. The Regiment was largely destroyed and had to be built up again. Over 700 officers and men went "over the top" at two o'clock in the afternoon, a fine afternoon and within a short time over 500 had been killed or wounded.

The article ends with this moving and patriotic passage.

So on this, the tenth anniversary of the Hohenzollern, we all think with loving tenderness of our lost friends and comrades, but also with ever enthusiastic admiration of their manhood and soildiership and with constantly deepening understanding that the policy for what they fought, suffered and died was worthy of the sacrifice. Those that died in the allied cause in the war died not in vain, but helped secure for the children they left behind and the new generations that constantly arrive that England should be England for ever.

We get the sense of importance from these two articles say about the attack on the Hohenzollern Redoubt on that fateful day, in searching for articles for the 50th anniversary in October 1965 there appeared to be no mention of the attack, had the war vanished from memory? No not really, it was still fresh in the minds of the survivors, however, from 1915-1965 the world had changed dramatically, and of course the Second World War of 1939-1945 had caused even more nationwide grief, and it was these new memories and mental scars that were haunting the people living in the 1960s. The social revolution in which the youth who grew up during the Second World War now had their own sense of identity, so an old fashioned war that had hardly any connection to them whatsoever would have seemed as distant to them as it may do with children now.

There was one instance where an article from August 2004 was shared to me by a man who will appear a little later in the memorials section of the book. Mark Watson Kindly sent me several articles and photographs to do with the Hohenzollern. What is interesting about the date of this article on the 89th anniversary was the fact, the last Great War survivors such as Harry Patch were finally telling their stories as they themselves knew they had little time left with us, harry died in 2009. The article was written by the late John Abberly, and is as follows.

Memories of our darkest day-500 soldiers dead.

It was an unforgettable sight- an old woman prancing along the pavement and shouting "Long live the Fifth North!" as soldiers of the North Staffordshire Regiment marched through stoke about 50 years ago.

I never discovered who she was, but my guess is that the old lady was a relative of one of the 500 men of the 5th Battalion North Staffords who died together in a few minutes on this area's blackest day in the First World War, or any other war.

During the Battle of Loos on October 13th, 1915 they charged the German lines and were mown down like flies by machine guns. Their CO, colonel Knight, led his men from the front and was one of the first to die.

I've seen a drawing by a sentinel artist, Wilf Sheard, showing men going over the top shouting "potters for ever!" and even kicking a football ahead of them. In most case it was the last words the uttered. Local communities in North Staffordshire were devastated by the scale of the tragedy. Hundreds of families in the potteries and Newcastle were bereaved. Many of the officers had grown up together as fellow pupils in Newcastle High School.

In 1915, deaths were reported daily and the life expectancy of a second Lieutenant was three weeks. But the impact of the slaughter of the Fifth North was so great that the army changed its policy, splitting up family Battalions on the front line to avoid such calamities.

In North Staffordshire, however, the sense pf bereavement lasted for a lifetime in some case. I met an elderly woman from Clayton who put a notice in the Sentinel on October 13th every year in memory of her father, even though she never knew him.

The article goes on to talk about other Great War stories and ends with, Ninety Years later, the old soldiers of the Fifth North haven't entirely faded away.

POTTERIES SOLDIER'S SKETCH OF THE CHARGE BY THE 1st-5th NORTH STAFFS.

A drawing by Private W. Sheard, of Fenton, as it appears, made on his mind during the gallant charge by the 1st 5th North Staffords. on October 13th last, when they rushed forward, crying "Potters for ever!"

[66]

We can only hope that there is coverage in local newspapers in Staffordshire, for the centenary which will of course take place on October 13th 2015.

---

[66] The Staffordshire Weekly Sentinel 20th November 1915 pp:7

Going back to yesteryear the list from 1917 of just a few of the casualties and how their families felt about them at the time, the people who loved them have long gone, in many cases, their homes too as the Staffordshire clean air act in the 1950s demolished many of the terraced houses they would have lived in. Their names are of course etched on the memorials in France but what about locally, have the men of Loos simply slipped away into the past?

The answer to that question is no. Nearly every community in Staffordshire has a reminder of the conflict that was raging 100 years ago. There are many in Staffordshire, every town in Stoke on Trent has one, some places even more, there is the Nicholson war memorial in leek which has a clock embedded into its tall structure. There are the countless church memorials, school and college memorials and also personal ones dedicated to individuals who fell, who came from wealthy backgrounds. They all had the same purpose, a place to gather, reflect and remember the fallen. At the time, just after the Great War, they were also places veterans could go to remember their fallen friends, so they didn't have to confide in their families, hence they became a coping mechanism. A place men could retreat if they ever found their experiences too overwhelming. Another reason memorials were erected was the harsh reality that not many of the fallen would return to be repatriated in their home towns, they became a sort of community grave stone where all could pay their respects. We now have the roll of honour, commemorating the North Stafford's who fell on October 13th 1915. For many years after the Great War, this list remained incomplete. Another question remains, where are our fallen heroes? Secondly where are they remembered? If you search the cemeteries of Staffordshire, you won't find a single grave with the remains of one of those who fell on October 13th 1915, because sadly they simply don't exist. As explained earlier in the book, the battle was utter chaos, and the deadly machine gunfire combined with the German shells falling all around them, at a rate not seen before, totally destroyed the remains of many of the fallen Staffordshire men. Whilst studying and exploring the cemeteries of Staffordshire the same dates appear, 1916 and 1918. Many of these men were brought back from the Somme and during the last campaign the North Stafford's were involved in, the German spring push, known as the Battle of St Quentin. As mentioned before, the Battle of Loos and most certainly the final attack against the Hohenzollern Redoubt have been confined to the shadows of the past, remembered only locally in the newspaper on the anniversary as seen previously with the emotive messages of loss. The Somme and Passchendaele saw greater losses and soon the story of Loos became forgotten as the war progressed. Much like modern events come and go. For example the downing of the MH17 Malaysian airliner on July 17th 2014. The story shocked the world, but only with the people directly affected did the story continue a month after nothing was heard in the news about it again. The same can be said for the sinking of the RMS Titanic in 1912, after the immediate coverage it did not appear in the news again until the discovery of the wreck. In local terms, as seen throughout this book, Hohenzollern came and went, but in Staffordshire it certainly was never forgotten, and if you look hard enough the names of the fallen and special memorials to those who fell are dotted around Staffordshire.

The following list shows a breakdown of the amount of men from the North Staffordshire Regiment buried in each cemetery in Staffordshire.

Hanley= 119

Longton 61

Burslem=57

Fenton= 20

Tunstall 26

Hartshill=92

Bucknall =2

Newcastle =19

Smallthorne=12

Burton on Trent=13

Wolstanton= 2

Uttoxeter = 5

Leek=1

Stone =2

Dresden =1

Normacot= 7

Eccelshall =2

Stafford =4

Forsbrook 2

Cheadle =2

Caverswall =2

Not one of these men fell on October 13th 1915, in fact only one man from the North Staffordshire Regiment men ever made it back to England for burial. That man was Private Arthur Mollart who died of wounds in a London hospital on October 26th 1915, and he is buried in Kensal Green cemetery in London.

If you were to find the fallen of Loos, Northern France would be the place to go. The commonwealth war graves commission website allows us to look where the fallen men of Hohenzollern are buried. These men will not appear in alphabetical order, as the website gives their names in accordance to their grave location. The search is simply conducted by inputting the start and end dates as 13th October 1915 and typing North Staffordshire Regiment in the box labelled Regiment.

FOUQUIERES CHURCHYARD EXTENSION

Private 1573 John Joseph Holliday Neale of the 1/6th Battalion, of Lichfield.

Private 3872 Clarence Leckie of the 1/5th Battalion of Burslem.

ETAPLES MILITARY CEMETERY

Private 2697 Aaron Downs of the 1/5th Battalion, of Porthill, Stoke on Trent.

LOOS BRITISH CEMETERY

Captain Henry Akroyd Ridgeway 1/5th Battalion of Stone, Staffordshire.

CABARET-ROUGE BRITISH CEMETERY, SOUCHEZ

Private 2375 E L Plumb of the 1/6th Battalion

Lance corporal 2309 George William Baggaley of the 1/5th Battalion of Longton.

Sergeant 1501 F Kent of the 1/5th Battalion of Stoke.

Private 2428 Charles Henry Shuffelbottom of the 1/5th Battalion of Newcastle under Lyme.

Private 1981 A Clewlow of the 1/6th Battalion.

Lance corporal 3864 B R Shorthouse of the 1/5th Battalion.

Private 2883 Charles Brealey of the 1/6th Battalion of Burton on Trent.

Private 3954 T H Jones of the 1/5th Battalion of Hanley.

Private 3548 Henry John Ford of the 1/6th Battalion of Burton on Trent.

Private 1431 John Hayes of the 1/6th Battalion of Uttoxeter.

Private 2233 Harold Breeze of the 1/5th Battalion of Talke.

Sergeant 1338 A E Copeland of the 1/6th Battalion.

Private F J Evans of the 1/5th Battalion of Milton.

BULLY-GRENAY COMMUNAL CEMETERY, BRITISH EXTENSION

Private 2247 George Rowson of the 1/5th Battalion of Stone.

VERMELLES BRITISH CEMETERY

Lieutenant Oswald William Boddington of the 1/5th Battalion of Stone.

Private 2359 W F Clarke of the 1/5th Battalion.

Private 2767 Harry Allen Tudor of the 1/5th Battalion of Leek.

Private 2523 Charles Wood of the 1/6th Battalion of Burton on Trent.

Private 2971 J Worrall of the 1/6th Battalion.

LE TOURET MILITARY CEMETERY, RICHEBOUGH-L'AVOUE

Lance sergeant 12075 Jeremiah Barker of the 1/5th Battalion of Longton.

RUE-PETILLON MILITARY CEMETERY, FLEURBAIX

Private 1547 W Greenhough of the 1/5th Battalion.

Lance corporal 3385 C W Lane of the 1/5th Battalion of Newcastle under Lyme.

ST. MARY'S A.D.S. CEMETERY, HAISNES (The closest cemetery to the sight of the Hohenzollern redoubt)

Private 3333 John Booth of the 1/5th Battalion.

Private William Thomas Hand of the 1/5th Battalion.

Lance corporal 2937 Fred Hawley of the 1/5th Battalion of Fenton.

Private 401 W Heames of the 1/5th Battalion of Burslem.

Lance Corporal 1719 Henry Frederick Mallett of the 1/6th Battalion of Burton on Trent.

Sergeant 454 Leonard Millward of the 1/5th Battalion of Burslem.

Lance corporal 3219 Leonard Stokes of the 1/5th Battalion of Burslem.

Lance corporal 2774 Howard William Webster of the 1/5th Battalion of Newcastle under Lyme.

Private 3572 A Wharton of the 1/5th Battalion.

Private 3938 Arthur James Casey of the 1/5th Battalion of Stoke.

Private 3961 George Dwine of the 1/5th Battalion.

Private 1415 W Muston of the 1/5th Battalion.

SAILLY-LABOURSE COMMUNIAL CEMETERY EXTENSION

Captain James Hamilton Fleming of the 1/5th Battalion.

CANADIAN CEMETERY NO.2, NEUVILLE-ST. VAAST

Private 1550 Arthur Dale of the 1/5th Battalion of Kidsgrove, his brother Fred was not found.

Corporal 613 John Fitzjohn of the 1/5th Battalion of Stoke.

Sergeant 1522 Walter Washbrook of the 1/5th Battalion.

Sergeant Reginald Grimmitt stone of the 1/6th Battalion of Burton on Trent.

Shockingly that is it; just 43 men who fell on October 13th 1915 have known graves. 43 out of nearly 500 men. Every man who fell, both those who have known graves and those who don't are commemorated on the Loos memorial on panels 103-105. There will of course be many graves in these cemeteries with the words.

A SOLDIER OF THE GREAT WAR

KNOWN UNTO GOD.

How many of these unknown graves contain the remains of the casualties of Hohenzollern will never be known, and will more be discovered in years to come; only time will tell.

You have to look hard in Staffordshire to find links to the Stafford's and the attack on the Hohenzollern Redoubt. An impressive memorial is situated in Walsall town hall which was opened in 1902. Inside the town hall is an impressive organ, which is flanked by two paintings, one either side. They depict the South Staffordshire Regiments worst and what they consider their most successful day. One painting shows the South Stafford's advancing over the trench parapets. Above the painting it reads, The South Stafford's advancing the Hohenzollern Redoubt, and it is this image that depicts their worst day, although incorrectly depicted in steel helmets which were not introduced until 1916, none the less and impressive painting. On the other side of the organ is a second painting that depicts the South Stafford's storming the St Quentin Canal on September 29th 1918. This they believed was their most successful day. The centre of the memorial reads, to commemorate the never to be forgotten valour of the South Staffordshire Regiments in the Great War 1914-1918. In the centre of Stoke on Trent in the little town of Stoke, there is several impressive war memorials hidden away in Stoke town hall. In the entrance is an impressive memorial to the Boer war and next to that a small plaque listing three men who fought with the international brigade in the war against Fascism which took place from 1936-1939. As you proceed upstairs you walk past a large book locked away behind glass. This book is the original book that commemorates the men who were lost who fought in the North Staffordshire Regiment. The Front cover reads OUR GLORIOUS DEAD 1914-1918, and in the centre is the North Staffordshire cap badge. Even more moving is the stained glass window that stands proudly above the stair case. The beautiful window depicts and angle holding up the cap badge of the North Staffordshire Regiment up to the sky. What's special about this memorial is the dedication at the bottom.

To commemorate the Vth Battalion of the North Staffordshire Regiment (The Prince of Wales)

At the time of its dedication and instillation it must have drawn many memories for the survivors and families of those who died, not just Hohenzollern, but all the theatres of war that the 5th Battalion took part in. it seems a shame that it is now hidden away. In a conference hall there is another memorial to Major Cecil Wedgwood, the master potter and Great Great Grandson of Josiah Wedgewood who was killed in action on July the 3rd at the Battle of the Somme. Major Wedgwood was also the first mayor of Stoke on Trent, a few years before the Great War erupted.

The attack on the Hohenzollern Redoubt appears on two dedications on personal memorials in Stoke on Trent, one being in Burslem Cemetery. This is dedicated to Ernest Godfrey Thomas who had his own chapter. Thomas also appears in the Potteries Museum and art Galleries memorial which commemorates the former students of Hanley High school. The most information on a local memorial was kindly posted to me by a man called mark Watson. Ironically I had stumbled across one of the memorials on a quest to find my own relatives grave a few days before I received this letter.

Dear Mr Chevin.

In response to your request for information I enclose the following.

1) Memories of our darkest day-500 soldiers dead, an article by the late John Abberly from The Sentinel, august 2004.
2) The Dennitts memorial, church of the Holy evangelists, Normacot. Memorial to the Dennitts brothers one of whom was killed at the Hohenzollern Redoubt on October 13th 1915.
3) The grave stone of my great uncle at Longton Cemetery. He involved in the action of October 13th 1915, was wounded but survived. I never got the chance to meet him as he died just before I was born, if I find a photograph of him I will send you a copy to you.
This is a very worthwhile project that you have embarked on and I wish you all the success in this venture
Mark Watson.

Mr Watson's letter included to photographs, one of his Great uncles grave, who was called William Watson and on the back he wrote, William Watson served with the 5th North Stafford's and was wounded on October 13th 1915. The story goes that some of the soldiers received musical instruments as gifts, William Watson receiving an accordion, presented to them by the Lord Mayor. I do not know if this story was true but down the years I heard it was supposedly reported in the Sentinel at the time. The second photograph shows the Dennitts memorial. Which is adorned by a little union jack flag at the head of the memorial. The memorial is situated in Church of the Holy Evangelist's in Normacot. It is in this church where my own Great war Relative is buried, and also where my maternal Grandparents got married in the 1960s. The following is carved on the memorial.

Sacred To the Memory Of

LEWIS EDGAR DENNITTS

Dearly Beloved Husband Of

ALICE DENNITTS

Of Meir, Longton, Died 10th Aug 1922

Also of Cpl WILLIAM FREDERICK (Willie) DENNITTS.

6th North Staffs Regt Killed At the Hohenzollern Redoubt, France 13th Oct 1915 Aged 20 Years

Also of 2nd Lieut KENNETH JOHN WOLFE DENNITTS.

98th Squadron Royal Air Force Killed In Air Fight at Cambrai 3rd Sept 1918 Aged 18 Years.

"DEAR AND ONLY CHILDREN OF THE ABOVE, THY PURPOSE LORD WE CANNOT SEE"

TO THE HOHENZOLLERN REDOUBT.

STORMED BY THE NORTH MIDLAND DIVISION OCTOBER 13TH 1915.

Oh proud Hohenzollern, named after a king, you stood in your sullen might and a challenge to all British arms did fling. Caring little for pity and right.

Machine gunned and wired, your strength was well known, you were manned by a terrible crew, but little did you know, oh mighty Redoubt, what terrier men could do.

And you won't forget that October day, that sounded your funeral knell. Twas heard in the roar of the British guns, and the scream of the British shells. They broke your defences and splintered the wire, with a fury no power could stop, and you read your doom in that line of steel, when the boys went over the top.

And long you'll remember that Staffordshire rush, and the Lincoln and Leicester attack. Though you tore up their ranks with deadly fire, you failed to drive them back, though the ground was covered in British dead, they charged through your trenches, and then your last chance vanished when over the top came the Nott's and Derby men.

Oh men from the Midlands, the people back home are proud of your courage and skill and in long years to come, the tale of your deeds will echo in the Derbyshire hills, in the pottery towns and the valleys of the Trent and over the Lincolnshire fenn. They will tell the tale of the big Redoubt that was stormed by Terrier men.

Corporal Brand: 7th Nott's and Derby Regiment.

ROLL OF HONOUR

**1/5th Battalion|
The Prince of Wales's (North Staffordshire Regiment)**

Lieutenant-Colonel John Hall Knight V.D of Eccleshall,
aged 50

Captain James Hamilton Fleming Stone Bn HQ Adjutant

Captain Henry Ackroyd Ridgway of Stone

Captain Reginald Tavenor Johnson of Barlaston aged 36

Lieutenant Oswald William Boddington Stone Bn HQ M.G. Officer

Lieutenant Henry Robert Griffith Davies Alsager, Cheshire aged 28

Lieutenant Frank Bertram Mayer Alsager, Cheshire

Second-Lieutenant Nigel Bishop Stone aged 23

Second-Lieutenant Charles Arthur Lowndes Chesterton

LIEUT MELLOR, 1st-5th NORTH
STAFFORDSHIRE REGIMENT.

Second-Lieutenant Percy Mellor of Congleton, Cheshire aged 21

3620 Private Fred Abbotts of Burslem aged 32

3737 Private Mell Adlington of Wolstanton aged 33

Pte. E. AINSWORTH.

1602 Private Elijah Ainsworth of Stoke

3230 Private Ernest Alcock of Hanley aged 29

2818 Corporal George Allen of Longton

2918 Sergeant Cyril Allerton of Blythe Bridge aged 24

3908 Private John Arnold of Hanley

Pte. H. ASHMORE.

3929 Private Harry Ashmore of Talke aged 20

Sergt. S. ASHMORE.

1513 Sergeant Samuel Ashmore of Talke aged 22

2309 Lance-Corporal George Baggaley of Longton aged 19

2060 Sergeant William Bagguley of Fenton

3771 Private Ernest Ball of Dresden

2387 Private James Barker of Longton aged 17

2486 Private Alfred Barlow of Normacot aged 23 Brothers

3699 Private Thomas Barlow of Normacot aged 24 Brothers

Private James Edwin Bateman of Burslem

2138 Lance-Corporal Harry Beard of Longton aged 18

3660 Private Herbert Bennett of Willowbridge aged 19

3578 Private Arthur Beresford of Tunstall aged 20

3279 Private William Blakeman of Swynnerton

Pte J. BOOTH

3333 Private John Booth of Biddulph

Pte. J. BOULD.

2087 Private John Bould of Longton aged 22

1470 Private William Bowler of Burslem aged 23

Pte. BRAILSFORD.

3762 Private John Norris Brailsford of Hanley

2076 Private Samuel Brain of Longton aged 19

Pte H BREEZE
Killed

2233 Private Harold Breeze of Leeds, living in Butt Lane aged 18

167 Sergeant Thomas Brookes Longton

2637 Private Lewis Brough of Hanley aged 29

Pte. T. C. BROWN
Killed

3307 Lance-Corporal Joseph Brown Woore, of Cheshire

3989 Private John Brown of Smallthorne

Pte. H. BRUNT.

4020 Private Herbert Brunt of Fenton

Sapper W. J. BUTTRESS.

2365 Private William Buttress of Hanley aged 21

3334 Private Jonathan Washington Caum of Biddulph

3934 Private Anthony Campbell of Burslem aged21

3487 Private George Cartlidge of Longton aged 26

Pte. J. A. CASEY.

3938 Private James Casey of Brown Lees aged 22

1715 Private Albert Caulcott of Newcastle-under-Lyme

Pte. A. CLARKE.

1705 Private Arthur Clarke of Stoke

1538 Private Fred Clarke of Tunstall

Pte W CLARKE.
Killed

2359 Private William Clarke of Stoke aged 24

2033 Private Alfred Clayton of Stoke

3664 Private Samuel Colley of Burslem aged 23

3881 Private Norris George Cook of Newcastle-under-Lyme aged 19

3623 Private George Coomer of Newcastle-under-Lyme aged 21

2678 Lance-Corporal Fred Cope of Stoke

2319 Private Daniel Cotton of Longton aged 23

2811 C.Q.M.S. Algernon George Couzens of Chelsea living in Stone aged 24

3815 Private John Cresswell of Hanley aged 25

4017 Lance-Corporal Arthur Crompton of Longport

L-Cpl. A. CUMBERLIDGE.

2978 Lance-Corporal Arthur Cumberlidge of Longton aged 24

Pte. F. DALE. Killed.

Pte. A. DALE. Missing.

1550 Private Arthur Dale of Kidsgrove aged 21 Brothers

1541 Private Fred Dale of Kidsgrove aged 19 Brothers

1690 Lance-Corporal Fred Daniels of Hanley aged 23 Died of Wounds 16/10/15

4264 Private Percy Daniels of Burslem

2850 Lance-Corporal Frank Davenhill Stone

2560 Private Joshua Davies of Chesterton aged 19 Died of wounds 16/10/15

Pte. J. DAWSON.

2240 Private James Dawson of Stone aged 19

3691 Private John Deacon of Hanley aged 31

2504 Drummer Harold Deaville of Hanley aged 20

1091 Private Ernest Dewsnap of Trent Vale aged 18

460 Private Robert Dillon of Tunstall aged 20

Pte. F. DOWNING.

3931 Private Frank Downing of Kidsgrove aged 20

1414 Private Percy Durber of Chesterton

Pte. GEO. DWINE.

3961 Private George Dwine of Smallthorne

3156 Private James Edwards of Cobridge aged 20

L. CPL ARTHUR ELLIS, 1st 5th N S Regt.
Bomb Thrower, killed in action 13th
Oct. 1915, aged 27 years

2870 Lance-Corporal Arthur Ellis Alsager, of Cheshire aged 27

L.-Cpl. F. J. ENDACOTT.

2044 Private Thomas Endacott of Hanley aged 18

3848 Private Fred Evans of Smallthorne aged 23

613 Corporal Thomas Fitzjohn of Stoke aged 25

3783 Lance-Corporal Harry Flackett of Shelton aged 30

The following three were Brothers who fell together.

1323 Private Ernest Flannagan of Longton

3478 Private James Flannagan of Longton

2075 Private William Flannagan of Longton

Corpl E FLETCHER
Killed

2898 Lance-Corporal William Fletcher of Burslem

2627 Private Arthur Forrester of Hanley aged 32

3712 Private George Foster of Hanley

Bugler F. FORSYTHE

2528 Bugler Fred Forsythe of Fenton aged 19

2487 Private Richard Fullwood of Longton

3018 Private Thomas Gilbert of Nuneaton living in Stone

2139 Private Charles Gittins of Penkhull

2207 Private Arthur Glover of Stone aged 21 Brothers

1000 Private Graham Glover of Stone aged 23 Brothers

3403 Private Paul Glover of Cobridge aged 18

2819 Private Nathan Goodrum of Downsham Market, Norfolk

Pte. N. GOODWIN.

Private N Goodwin of Eccleshall

2817 Private Ashworth Gough of Hanley

4046 Private Sidney Grainger of Fenton aged 23

3676 Private William Gray of Hanley

1547 Private William Greenhough of Manchester living in Kidsgrove

2641 Private Oliver Hugh Griffiths of Bangor living in Newcastle-under-Lyme

3714 Lance-Corporal Fred Gwilliam of Stoke aged 21

2686 Private Robert Hall of Alsager, Cheshire aged 24

3530 Private Thomas Hall of Newcastle-under-Lyme aged 19

1480 Private George Hammonds of Burslem Died of wounds 19/10/15

2635 Corporal Joseph Hand of Stoke cousins

3956 Private Thomas Hand of Stoke cousins

3377 Private Harry Handley of Hanley aged 21

3593 Lance-Corporal David Harrison of Hanley

2937 Lance-Corporal Fred Hawley of Fenton aged 24

3600 Private Ernest Hayes of Fenton

3077 Private Arnold Haylett of Burslem 20 Died of wounds 25/10/15

Pte. JIM HEAMES

401 Private William Heames of Burslem

1536 Private Ernest Heath of Butt Lane

2498 Private Fred Heath of Fenton aged 19

3258 Private Jack Hill of Longton aged 20

4013 Private Joseph Hodgkinson of Norton-le-Moors

3580 Private John Hodson of Dresden aged 19

2856 Private Charles Holgate of Hanley

3402 Private Fred Hood of Burslem aged 26

Pte C E HUDSON

2776 Private Charles Hudson of Hanley aged 18

1682 Private James Hulme of Longton

Pte. J. HUMPHRIES.

1493 Private John Humphreys of Burslem aged 19

3511 Private Joseph Humphreys of Burslem

2058 Private William Hurst of Longton aged 23

2944 Lance-Sergeant Philip Irwin of Stone aged 21 Died of wounds 14/10/15

4072 Private Thomas Issard of Hanley aged 20 Died of wounds 15/10/15

1743 Private James Jennings of Silverdale aged 22

Pte. GEO. JONES.

2812 Private George Jones of Stone

2339 Private John Jones of Hanley

2688 Sergeant Sydney Jones of Newcastle-under-Lyme aged 32

3954 Private Thomas Jones of Hanley aged 30

1779 Private Thomas Johnson of Newcastle-under-Lyme

3757 Private Charles Kelter of Shelton aged 27

3366 Lance-Corporal William Kennerley of Biddulph

1501 Sergeant Frank Kent of Kidsgrove aged 35

2998 Lance-Corporal Harry Landon of Hanley

3385 Lance-Corporal Charles Lane of Newcastle-under-Lyme aged 22

2669 Corporal Lewis Latimer of Longport

3031 Private Cecil Lawton of Stoke

3872 Private Clarence Leckie of Liverpool, living in Burslem aged 22

2155 Acting Sergeant William Leese of Newcastle-under-Lyme aged 20

2121 Private Bertie Leigh of Hanley Died of wounds 19/10/15

3344 Lance Sergeant Arnold Lewis of Barbados living in Newchapel

3146 Private Duncan McClarence of Newcastle upon Tyne living in Dresden Died of wounds 26/10/15

2912 Lance-Corporal Sydney Denny Marsden of Stoke

2393 Private Fred Marshall of Hanley aged 18

2940 Lance-Corporal Edward Massey of Hanley aged22

2659 Private John Matthews of Bucknall aged 21

3892 Private Samuel Mellor of Milton aged 19

3039 Private Edward Miller of Hanley

454 Corporal Leonard Millward of Burslem aged 38

Pte. F. MITCHELL.

1412 Private Fred Mitchell of Newcastle-under-Lyme aged 23

Pte. C. MITFORD.

3251 Private Christopher Mitford of Alsager, Cheshire aged22

Pte A MOLLART

1900 Private Arthur Mollart of Burslem aged 19 Died of wounds 26/11/15

4023 Private George Morgan of Fenton

3658 Private Harry Morrey of Hanley aged 19

2066 Private Edward Morris of Longton

3343 Private William Morris of Biddulph

2600 Private Gilbert Moulton of Silverdale aged 19

Pte W MUSTON
killed

1415 Private William Muston of Knutton aged34

927 Private William Nicholls of Stone

3597 Private Harold Nixon of Penkhull

3885 Private William Parkes of Longton

3022 Private George Parr of Newcastle-under-Lyme 25 Brothers

3277 Private Reginald Parr of Newcastle-under-Lyme 21 Brothers

1479 Private Noah Pedley of Burslem

3280 Private John Perks of Swynnerton aged 27

3972 Private William Plant of Smallthorne aged 19

2241 Private Lewis Plimmer of Stone aged 20

Pte A POWELL
killed

3701 Private Alfred Powell of Hanley

3971 Private William Prosser of Burslem aged 24 Died of wounds 17/10/15

2177 Private Percy Ralphs of Newcastle-under-Lyme aged 22

4068 Sergeant Fred Ratcliffe of Porthill aged 23

3545 Private Harold Ravensdale of Stoke

3520 Private John Reade of Burslem aged 24

Lance Corpl REEVES
Wounded

3353 Lance-Corporal John Reeves of Brindley Ford aged 26

3245 Private Harry Ridge of Longton aged 25

3996 Private Thomas Rigby Lawton, of Cheshire aged 22

58 Lance-Sergeant Arthur Roberts of Shelton

3669 Private George Roberts of Burslem

3492 Lance-Corporal David Robinson of Biddulph

2614 Private Thomas Robinson of Cobridge

Pte T R RODEN
Died

3454 Private Thomas Roden of Longton aged 16

2842 Private Philip Rowe of Hanley aged 21

3442 Private Rowland Rowley of Leigh aged 20

2247 Private George Rowson of Stone aged 23

607 Sergeant Fred Sant of Stoke aged 31

333 Private Charles Sharman of Burslem

2716 Acting Corporal Robert Shaw of Newcastle-under-Lyme

3792 Private Tom Shaw of Crewe, Cheshire aged 28

2097 Private William Shaw of Burslem aged 18

Private William Henry Shaw Fenton 20 Missing

Pte. H. SHELDON.
Killed.

3072 Private Harry Sheldon of Shelton

4214 Private Albert Sherrat of Burslem

3330 Private Robert Sherrat of Biddulph aged 20

2700 Private William Sherry of Stoke aged 22

3864 Lance-Corporal Benjamin Shorthouse of Stoke

P o C SHUFFLEBOTHAM

It is not known which of the following two Charles Shuffelbotham's this is

3038 Private Charles Shufflebotham of Newcastle-under-Lyme aged 21

2428 Private Charles Henry Shufflebotham of Goldenhill aged 19

2306 Private George Shufflebotham of Cobridge aged 34

2180 Private Joseph Shuker of Stoke aged 23

Pte. A. SKELLERN.

4058 Private Alfred Skellern of Longton

1515 Corporal Alexander Smith of Burslem aged25

1575 Private James Smith of Stone aged 21

1832 Private Robert Smith of Tunstall

Pte R T SNAPE

2765 Private Ralph Twist Snape of Newcastle-under-Lyme aged 24 Died of wounds 17/10/15

3219 Lance-Corporal Leonard Stokes of Burslem

3639 Private Alfred Sutton of Shelton

3396 Private Arthur Talbot of Goldenhill

Lce Cpl H. TALBOT.
Wounded.

3244 Lance-Corporal Harry Talbot of Longton died of wounds at an unknown date aged25

2951 Lance-Sergeant Ernest Thomas of Wolstanton aged 25

1333 Private John Thomas of Longton

3905 Private James Tilestone of Stoke

Pte W H 100 H
 Tuld

2081 Private William Tooth of Longton aged 18

3733 Private James Townsend of Stoke aged 31

2767 Private Harry Tudor of Leek aged 21

3802 Private John Tunnicliffe of Hanley

3425 Private James Tunstall of Stoke aged 16

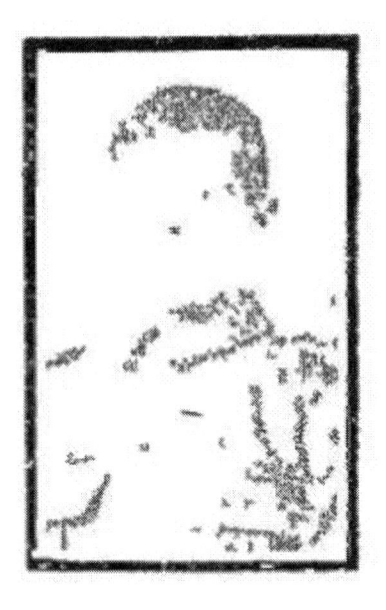

Pte. E. J. TURNER.

3199 Private Edward Turner of Etruria aged 28

1070 Lance-Sergeant William Turnock of Penkhull

1495 Private Alfred Tyler of Burslem

1636 Private John Walker of Fenton aged 19

1298 Sergeant Richard Walker of Shelton aged 22

378 Lance-Corporal James Wardle of Burslem aged 25

Pte. GEO. WARHAM.
Wounded.

1428 Private George Warham of Bignall End aged 23

1522 Sergeant Walter Washbrook of Oxford living in Tunstall

192 C.S.M. Henry Washington of Fenton aged 43

2774 Lance-Corporal William Webster of Newcastle-under-Lyme aged 28

3572 Private Albert Wharton of Tunstall

2583 Lance-Corporal John Whitehouse of Tunstall aged 35

1725 Private John William Whitehouse Silverdale 22

2418 Private Thomas Whittle of Newcastle-under-Lyme aged 18

2598 Private Elijah Williams of Newcastle-under-Lyme

2940 Private Ernest Williams of Burslem

4061 Private James Williams of Silverdale aged 20

Corpl. WILLIE.

3538 Corporal Colonel Fenton aged 17

3192 Private John Wilson of Burton-on-Trent

3091 Lance-Corporal Fred Woodcock of Burslem

3945 Private Henry Yarwood of Smallthorne

2936 Private Alfred Yorke of Alsager, Cheshire aged 24

1/6th Battalion
The Prince of Wales's (North Staffordshire Regiment)

Captain Oswald Joseph Bamford of Uttoxeter aged 38

Captain John Jenkinson of Tamworth aged 33

Second-Lieutenant Ostcliffe Harold Beaufort of Oaklands Park aged 22

Second-Lieutenant John Blanchard aged 35

Second-Lieutenant Andrew Stewart Fox Beaconsfield, of Buckinghamshire aged 21

Second-Lieutenant Horace Neville Hartley of Stone aged 26

Second-Lieutenant John Philip Edmund Owens of Burton-on-Trent

1648 Sergeant Leslie Cecil Atkinson of Burton-on-Trent aged 21

2329 Private William Bagnall of Horninglow aged 32

3072 Private Charles Bailey of Burton-on-Trent aged 25

2770 Private Sidney Bennett of Burton-on-Trent

1273 Private George Birch of Burton-on-Trent aged 22

1823 Private Joseph Blackwell of Uttoxeter

1430 Private Harry Bloor of Uttoxeter aged 31

1817 Private Fred Bott of Lichfield

2883 Private Charles Brearley of Burton-on-Trent

2 C.S.M. John Lewis Brindley of Burton-on-Trent

1428 Private William Brough of Uttoxeter Died of wounds 14/10/15

2844 Lance-Corporal Daniel Carlisle of Burton-on-Trent aged 18

2421 Private John Carvell of Burton-on-Trent

2182 Private Bertram Chilton of Burton-on-Trent aged 18

3364 Private John Christelow of Burton-on-Trent

2369 Private James Clack of Burton-on-Trent aged 18

1796 Drummer John Clarke of Burton-on-Trent aged 18

2119 Private Reginald Clarke of Rugeley aged 19

1981 Private Alfred Clewlow Stafford

1338 Lance - Sergeant Arthur Copeland of Burton-on-Trent

867 Sergeant George Cutler of Burton-on-Trent

1812 Private Harold Curzon Uttoxeter B

1506 Private James Deakin of Rugeley

3263 Corporal William Dennitts of Longton aged 20

A memorial to William Dennitts is situated in the Holy Evangelist church in Normacot and mentions the Hohenzollern Redoubt.

2294 Private William Duffin of Stafford

3162 Private Bernard Eames Swadlincote of Derby

2365 Private George Eaton of Burton-on-Trent aged 19

1857 Private Charles Edwards of Burton-on-Trent aged 21

2821 Lance-Corporal Leonard Ewers of Horninglow aged 23

104 Sergeant William Eyre of Burton-on-Trent aged 28

1196 Private James Fisher of Rugeley aged 28

2632 Lance-Corporal Fred Ford of Willenhall

3458 Private John Ford of Burton-on-Trent aged 23

2664 Acting Corporal James Perkin Fradley of Uttoxeter aged 38

It was this man who tried to save Captain Bamford.

2398 Private Harry Gadsby of Burton-on-Trent aged 23

3607 Private William Gent of Woodville, Derby aged 31

1762 Private Fred Geohegan of Stafford

1630 Private Percy German of Burton-on-Trent A 21 Died of wounds 17/10/15

2345 Private Harry Goodhead of Burton-on-Trent aged 18

40 Private John Gough of Burton-on-Trent died of wounds 14/10/15

2349 Private Harry Grimley of Rolleston-on-Dove aged 30

1405 Private Ernest Hall of Lichfield aged 26

2470 Private Thomas Wells Hallam of Burton-on-Trent aged 28

1431 Private John (Dan) Hayes of Uttoxeter aged 19

1495 Private William Heath of Burton-on-Trent aged 22

1803 Private John Hodgkins of Lichfield

2344 Private Silvester Benjamin Hodgkins of Burton-on-Trent aged 21

2042 Private William Holley of Stapenhill died of wounds 24/10/15

1573 Private John Joseph Holliday Neale of Lichfield aged 23

2673 Private William Holmes of Uttoxeter aged 27

2310 Private Rupert Inwood of Burton-on-Trent aged 19

3099 Private Joseph Jevons of Burton-on-Trent

3039 Private Francis John Kelham of Stapenhill aged 24

1818 Private Norman Lomas Tideswell, of Derby aged 25

1649 Private Samuel McMillan of Burton-on-Trent aged 19

3393 Private John Makin of Burton-on-Trent

1719 Lance-Corporal Fred Mallet of Burton-on-Trent aged 22

1643 Private Herbert Marler of Burton-on-Trent

2311 Private Walter Mayne of Burton-on-Trent died of wounds 19/10/15

1988 Private Frank Marsh of Elford head 22 died of wounds 14/10/15

2224 Private Ernest Mason of Amington aged 19 died of wounds 15/10/15

1573 Private John Neale of Lichfield aged 23

3433 Private Alfred Neild of Doveridge, Derby

2072 Private Walter Neville of Lichfield

574 Sergeant William Norton of Burton-on-Trent

2801 Private Fred Ottewell of Burton-on-Trent

2375 Private Ernest Plumb of Tutbury

3288 Private William Redfern of Burton-on-Trent

2498 Private Herbert Richardson of Uttoxeter aged 23

1888 Private Thomas Richardson of Tutbury aged 21

2903 Private Percy Sawyer of Burton-on-Trent aged 18

2270 Private John Shale of Stafford

2544 Private Ernest Smith of Tamworth aged 29 died of wounds 22/10/15

2121 Private Arthur Smith of Doveridge, Derby

2508 Private Sampson Smith of Uttoxeter

2187 Private William Stockwell of Burton-on-Trent

2330 Sergeant Reginald Stone of Burton-on-Trent aged 26

2515 Private Sydney Stubbs of Uttoxeter aged 25

2424 Private Harry Sutton of Burton-on-Trent aged 28

2963 Private Walter Tack of Burton-on- Trent

2522 Private Bertram Taft of Uttoxeter aged 17

2472 Private Leonard Taylor of Burton-on-Trent

2362 Lance-Corporal Leslie Harry Tooby of Burton-on-Trent aged 25

2994 Private William Tyson of Uttoxeter aged 20

1953 Private Joseph Wainwright of Tamworth aged 21

350 Sergeant Frank Wallbank D.C.M. of Rugeley aged 29

1922 Private James Walters of Stafford

3026 Private Edward Washington of Burton-on-Trent B

1523 Private Tom Williams of Hopwas

3367 Private Thomas Wilson of Burton-on-Trent

2823 Private William Witherow of Burton-on-Trent aged 19

2523 Private Charles Wood of Uttoxeter aged 40

3281 Private Joseph Woodhead of Burton-on-Trent aged 29

3157 Private Arthur Woodyet of Burton-on-Trent aged 28

3270 Acting Corporal Thomas Woolley of Burton-on-Trent aged 20

2971 Private James Worrall of Tutbury

2631 Private William Worrall of Stafford aged 29 died of wounds 16/10/15

2605 Private Charles Wright of Lichfield aged 40 Died of wounds 15/10/15

"Wednesday October 13th of this year, is in North Staffordshire a never to be forgotten date in the history of the Great War. On this day the distinguished gallantry of the 5th Battalion North Staffordshire Regiment was inscribed on the scroll of honour in letters of blood and tears of anguish, on this sacrificial day our own brave boys showed themselves worthy of the best traditions of the British Army at a cost which has brought sorrow to many Staffordshire homes"

The Staffordshire weekly sentinel

October 30th 1915

Callan Chevin.

Made in the USA
Lexington, KY
15 June 2015